JOHN

A Devotional Commentary

JOHN

A Devotional Commentary

Meditations on the Gospel According to St. John

GENERAL EDITOR
Leo Zanchettin

The Word Among Us
9639 Doctor Perry Road
Ijamsville, Maryland 21754
www.wau.org
ISBN: 0-932085-40-7

Scripture quotations are from the Revised Standard Version of the Bible, copyright 1946, 1952, 1971, by the Division of Christian Education of the National Council of the Churches of Christ in the U.S.A. Used by permission.

Cover:
Saint John the Evangelist by Hans Memling, 1433-1494.
Detail from the right wing of the triptych of John Donne,
National Gallery, London
Photograph © Eric Lessing/Art Resource, NY
Cover design by David Crosson

Made and printed in the United States of America.

Foreword

Dear Friends in Christ:

In the prologue to his gospel, John tells us that the eternal Son of God took on human flesh and lived among us as a man (John 1:14). Then, as he unfolds his gospel, John shows us what happens when God comes to visit his people in so personal a way: The lame walk, the blind see, and the dead are raised to life (5:8-9; 9:6-7; 11:43-44).

John is careful, however, not to talk only about Jesus' miracles. In page after page, he shows us the love of a God who wants to re-create us in his divine image and likeness. No matter where we look, we encounter Jesus inviting us to turn to him so that we can receive his life within our hearts. This is a gospel of transformation: from flesh to spirit (3:6), from darkness to light (8:12), from death to life (5:24). Just as he spoke to Lazarus, Jesus asks each of us to come out of the tomb of our old life and come to him.

It was with these thoughts in mind that we set out to put together this devotional commentary on the Gospel of John. We believe that as we come to Jesus in prayer and ask him to speak to us through scripture, our lives will be transformed. Jesus is the Word of God (1:1). His words have the power to pierce our hearts and fill them with love (6:63). All he asks is that we receive his words with a heart like the beloved disciple in this gospel—in quiet surrender as we rest our heads against Jesus' breast. Our prayer is that the meditations in this book will encourage you to take up this position of faith, so that you may come to know the "grace and truth" that only Jesus can give (1:14).

We want to thank everyone who has made this commentary possible. Many of the meditations produced here were initially developed for *The Word Among Us* monthly publication, and we want to thank the writers of these meditations for granting us permission to reprint their work. We also want to thank Fr. Joseph Mindling, O.F.M. Cap., Joe Difato, and Hallie Riedel for their considerable contributions. May the Lord abundantly bless them all.

Leo Zanchettin
General Editor

Table of Contents

An Introduction to the Gospel According to John

By Fr. Joseph A. Mindling, O.F.M. Cap.

The Gospel according to John is the fourth and final New Testament summary of the crucial moments of Jesus' public life—an account wonderfully enhanced with rich theological reflections. Although modern scholars have been unable to reach consensus about the different people who might have been involved in the process of composing and editing this book, ancient tradition links these inspired memoirs to an unnamed figure mentioned only in the pages of this text: the "Beloved Disciple."

Called to Be Followers and Friends

The task of any disciple is learning by imitating the master. Consequently, this classical connection between the gospel and a favorite member of Jesus' band of followers offers an attractive key for anyone who wants to get the most out of reading these inspired pages today. In fact, a close examination of the text confirms that it was deliberately designed for readers seeking to deepen their knowledge and understanding of Jesus, the unique Teacher sent by the heavenly Father.

But this gospel is about more than just increasing our "information":

> Indeed, there are also many other things which Jesus did. If every one of them were written down, I suppose that the world itself could not contain the books that would be written. . . . But these are written that you may believe that Jesus is the Christ, the Son of God, and that believing you may have life in his name. (21:25; 20:31)

Although it accurately preserves memories of some of the most important teachings and actions of Jesus, the Gospel of John was not intended to be a documentary or a simple biography. It is, rather, an extended narrative essay, an album of selected scenes from Jesus' life, crafted for those who are called to be "Beloved Disciples" themselves. Ultimately, John's account was intended to be an invitation to embrace Jesus' offer of friendship and an aid in deepening that relationship with our Savior and Friend.

A Unique Perspective

By the time this gospel was composed at the end of the first century, the early Christian community had already been enriched with other accounts of Jesus' life, circulated under the prestigious names of missionaries like Mark and Luke and the apostle Matthew. All three of these gospels shared a similar approach. They are basically collections of brief stories, many of which are repeated in two or more of them. Each version of the Good News effectively draws together diverse episodes into an engaging stream of events. Each one, in its own way, helps readers to enter into what the first apostles experienced as they lived and worked with Jesus.

The Gospel of John followed this precedent in many ways. It too weaves together descriptions of Jesus' deeds and preaching in Galilee and Judea, and it provides detailed information about the Last Supper, the crucifixion, and the resurrection. However, John also diverges from this pattern by forging new and distinctive vantage points for his readers, to help them get more deeply in touch with Jesus' mysterious magnetism.

For example, while the synoptic gospels record that Jesus spoke of numerous moral requirements, John focuses almost exclusively on Jesus' command to love one another. Matthew, Mark, and Luke all include a brief summary of the institution of the Eucharist when they describe the final meal before the passion. Instead, John chooses to report Jesus' washing the feet of his disciples, his trusting prayer, and the discourse about his own unique relationship with God the Father.

The first three gospels relate many wonders that Jesus performed —miracles which they describe as acts of power. John recounts only seven, but his detailed storytelling draws readers into a more penetrating meditation on the fuller, more personal meaning of these "signs" (2:11; 6:2; 12:37). Of course, John is aware of how startling these activities of Jesus were, but he also wants his readers to see them as pointing back to the wonder worker who performed them.

Thus, all the gospels include reports about Jesus' restoring vision to blind persons. Matthew, for example, recounts more than half a dozen such cases. John, on the other hand, only selects one, but he devotes an entire chapter to Jesus' transformation of the life of a blind beggar (9:1-41). Forced by hostile religious authorities to reflect repeatedly on his healing, this formerly sightless young person slowly comes to understand his amazing cure as a sign directing him to the Stranger who had shown him compassion. At first, he did not even ask his healer's name. By the end of the passage, however, his ability to see physically was combined with new inner sight and he could acclaim: "Lord, I believe" (9:38).

A Deepening Acquaintance

This unnamed beggar can serve as a role model for all of us in approaching John's Gospel. Like him—and like others whom we see interacting with Jesus in its pages—our quest is to grapple with the puzzle of who Jesus is. On the one hand, it seems easy to answer such a question with something like a name or a title or a short job description. In fact, several such replies can be found right in the gospel itself: Messiah, Lamb of God, Son of Man, Good Shepherd, and Savior.

These responses represent a fine start, and they are accurate, as far as they go. Yet we are all aware that there is another much more profound way of answering this question. Old friends, coworkers, and even spouses can know each other's names and biographical data but still not really be in touch with who their companions are. The fourth gospel takes up this identity question as it reveals important truths about Jesus, but it also reminds us that there is much to know and much that can be misunderstood.

The opening prologue (1:1-18) plunges right into this project, stating poetically but decisively that Jesus is divine. His eternal origin is the glorious, life-giving light of the Godhead, and through him everything in the universe was brought into existence. Jesus is the living Expression of the Source of being. He is the Voice of divine self-disclosure. No other gospel contains such bold and explicit statements about the status of Jesus prior to the moment when the Word became flesh and dwelt among us.

The human characteristics of Jesus depicted in John—his physical reality and emotions—are also instruments of revelation. "Anyone who has seen me," he tells his disciples, "has seen the Father" (14:9). Only John gives us poignant details about the crown of thorns and the nail wounds, about the Savior's tearful grieving over the death of Lazarus, and about his grilling fish on the beach (11:35; 19:2 20:25; 21:9). The mysterious com-penetration of the human and the divine is proclaimed from the very first chapter and colors our perception of everything else that is reported about what Jesus said and did. But John shows that those who encountered him in the course of his ministry responded to what they saw in very different ways.

Individual Encounters

At first ignorant of Jesus' true identity, John the Baptist is led, through witnessing the descent of the Spirit, to announce "This is the Son of God!" On the contrary, Nathanael's first reaction is conditioned by a prejudice that could have prevented their meeting at all: "Can anything good come out of Nazareth?" A personal exchange with the Nazarene himself brings Nathanael to a complete change of heart, but only after Jesus reveals his already intimate knowledge of this skeptical young fellow from Cana. As a result, Nathanael would eventually become one of the apostolic witnesses of the risen Lord (1:31,34,46; 21:1-14).

In several instances, conversations with Jesus led to a similar spark of faith, which he both affirmed and fanned into flame. John preserves reassuring memories of Jesus giving ordinary persons like ourselves unhurried time and attention based on their special circumstances. He draws out a feisty, middle-aged divorcee in Samaria (4:1-42). He grants late-night appointments to an undercover consort who serves by day on the Sanhedrin Council (3:1-15). He consoles and challenges Martha in her wave of disillusionment over the untimely death of her brother (11:17-27). As they speak with Jesus, each of these individuals deals in his or her own way with the same underlying questions: Who is this Person? Who is he for me?

Throughout the gospel, the evangelist gradually but deliberately heightens our sensitivity to new layers of meaning concealed within seemingly ordinary words and expressions—living water, being born, bread from heaven, truth, and belief in the resurrection

(4:11; 3:3; 6:33; 8:32; 11:25). One of the most important double meanings running through this gospel is John's paradoxical understanding of the cross as both ignominious and victorious: " 'And I, if I be lifted up from the earth, will draw all things to myself.' Jesus said this signifying by what death he was to die" (12:31-32). This gospel is certainly a treasure trove for those who think that "life" left unexamined is not worth living.

Opposition that Reveals the Truth

In more tranquil settings, John also includes episodes in which Jesus encounters fierce antagonism. Still, even his most determined opponents can voice harshly critical statements which, with unwitting irony, actually express profound theological truths:

> Some said, "He is the Christ: but some objected, "Can the Christ come from Galilee? Does not the scripture say that it is of the offspring of David, and from Bethlehem, the village where David lived, that the Christ is to come?" (7:40-42)

In this gospel, even maliciously intended remarks can foreshadow important Christian beliefs about the saving power of the sufferings of Jesus:

> Caiphas, being high priest that year, said to them: "You know nothing at all, nor do you reflect that it is expedient for us that one man die for the people, instead of the whole nation perishing." This, however, he said not of himself, but being high priest that year, he prophesied that Jesus was to die for the nation—and not only for the nation, but that he might gather into one the children of God who were scattered abroad. (11:49-52)

A Gospel to Be Read in the Spirit

Both first-time readers of this gospel and those for whom it is an old favorite can testify to its ability to provide consolation and challenge. Unfortunately, it is still possible to react negatively or apathetically when the word of God strikes a personal chord in us—just as some reacted to Jesus' own preaching:

> "Do you take offense at this?" he asked. . . "It is the spirit that gives life, the flesh is of no avail; the words that I have spoken to you are spirit and life. But there are some of you that do not believe." . . . After this, many of his disciples drew back and no longer walked with him. (6:61-66)

If, on the contrary, we feel the power of this gospel drawing us more deeply into the mystery it enshrines, we should realize that we are actually sharing in the fulfillment of Jesus' words on the night before he died:

> I still have many things to say to you. . . . When the Spirit of Truth comes, he will guide you into all truth. The Paraclete, the Holy Spirit, whom the Father will send in my name, will teach you all things and bring to your remembrance all that I have said to you. (16:13; 14:25-26)

Saint Clement of Alexandria wisely described the Gospel according to John as a "spiritual" gospel. He meant this, not in the sense of "immaterial" or "ethereal," but as "written for those who are empowered by the Spirit of Truth to understand and to open their hearts to the revelation it contains." With this spiritual illumination, the fourth gospel continues to address us with the welcoming invitation Jesus offered to the two curious disciples of John the Baptist who came to learn more about him: "Come and see!" (1:39).

Meeting Jesus in the Gospels

By Joe Difato

What would you do if you were given the chance to meet any five people you wanted? Who would be on your list? A great scientist, like Albert Einstein or Jonas Salk? Maybe a sports legend, like Babe Ruth or Michael Jordan? What about a very holy person, like Mother Teresa or Pope John Paul II? Or maybe a world leader, like Queen Elizabeth or Mahatma Gandhi? Undoubtedly, they would be people whom you have read about in a book or seen stories about on television. You might even know a lot about their lives and achievements. Still, there's something different about having personal meetings with them that no amount of learning can replace.

Each of us would probably have different people on our list, but one principle would be the same for all of us. We would all choose people whom we felt had something to offer us. It might be their ability to teach us something new. We might hope that they could tell us the secret to their success. Or maybe we feel that meeting them could give us a greater sense of purpose for our lives.

Scripture tells us that many different people sought Jesus out and wanted to meet him—people who knew that he had something very valuable to offer them. Some came because they heard of the miraculous healings he had been performing. Others were moved by a longing for God in their hearts. Still others wondered whether he might really be the Messiah they had been awaiting. Certainly some were compelled by his preaching—his message of mercy, love, and hope from the Father in heaven.

For these people, it was not enough just to hear about Jesus or to admire him from a distance. They had to experience him firsthand.

The Common Link: Revelation

The one common factor at work in all these people was that the Holy Spirit had enabled them to see Jesus as more than just an ordinary man. When Jesus asked his disciples who they thought he was, Peter replied, "You are the Christ, the Son of the living God" (Matthew 16:16). Jesus commended Peter and told him, "Flesh and blood has not revealed this to you, but my Father in heaven" (16:17). Peter thought the words came only from his understanding—and to a degree they did—but Jesus told him that the conviction behind the truth, the heart-changing revelation that he proclaimed, came from God.

St. Paul knew a similar experience. He told the Christians in Corinth, "No one can say, 'Jesus is Lord,' except by the Holy Spirit" (1 Corinthians 12:3). Paul knew that his experience of Jesus did not come from his own reasoning or from the words of other people but "through a revelation of Jesus Christ" (Galatians 1:12), and he longed for all people to have a similar revelation.

What was true for Paul and Peter is true for us as well, and it can happen in a powerful way when we read the gospels. Each of us can know Jesus personally, not just as a figure from history or as the subject of theological study, but as a personal Lord and Savior. We can know him as a friend and brother whose love can heal us and deliver us from all our sins.

A Personal Encounter through the Gospels

While it is helpful to read the gospels so that we can learn about Jesus, we should remember that the Bible is only made up of paper and ink. The words printed on its pages are just like the words in any other book—unless these words are brought to life by the Holy Spirit.

Do you believe that it is possible to know every historical fact about Jesus and yet not know him personally? Do you believe that it is possible to know every fact about Jesus' culture, his friends, and his enemies, and still not know his mercy and saving love? This is why it is vital that we read the gospels with hearts open to the Holy Spirit. Without the Spirit, it would be just like reading a good book about someone on our list of five people. It wouldn't satisfy our deepest needs. This is why it is such good news that we can meet Jesus every time we pray (Luke 11:9-13), receive the Eucharist (John 6:35,56), repent (Matthew 5:6), and care for the needy (Matthew 25:37-40). We can meet Jesus every time we read the gospels (Romans 10:17).

The Holy Spirit promises that when we spend time dwelling on the gospels, they will come to life for us and we will see God working in us—just as Peter did when he confessed Jesus as the Messiah. We will see the wisdom of God flowing into our lives, just as Paul promised the Corinthians (1 Corinthians 2:6-16). Best of all, we will meet Jesus personally. Let's take a look at how this can happen.

A Prayerful Reading of the Gospels

Think about the way your mind works on any given day. Every day, you use your imagination to help you plan what you will do, solve a problem, or cook a meal. You imagine the result of your planning with your "mind's eye" and then, as you perform that activity, you watch it unfold with your "physical eye." Just as this happens on a natural level, so your imagination can function on a spiritual level as you invite the Holy Spirit to fill you with his power and grace

The next time you listen to or read the gospels, use your imagination. Try to picture the scene, grasp the temperament of the people involved, and feel the atmosphere around Jesus. With your mind's eye, try to envision what the passage is describing.

Next, ask the Holy Spirit to open your heart to the wisdom of the passage. Ask him to help you see this passage as God wants us to see it. It's when you do this that your spiritual capacities are awakened and your imaginings take on a whole new dimension.

Take a look, for example at Jesus' encounter with the woman caught in adultery (John 8:1-11). Take a moment to read this passage quietly. Now, place yourself in the middle of the scene as John describes it. Try to imagine the woman's fear as she stands before her accusers. Look at the scribes and Pharisees who brought her before Jesus and try to feel their anger and indignation. Try to get a sense of the love that Jesus had, both for this woman and for her accusers.

As you pray through this passage, ask the Holy Spirit to open you up to new dimensions of the story. Don't be surprised if you experience new and different things happening in you. You may be filled with a new compassion for those bound in prostitution. You may have a taste of the depths of Jesus' forgiveness and love for you personally and find yourself filled with a desire to love God more. You may realize that, like the Pharisees, you are quick to condemn or easily provoked when confronted with your own sin. Maybe you feel moved to show mercy in a very practical way to the poor and outcast. As scripture says, there is no telling what God is prepared to do for those who seek him and love him (1 Corinthians 2:9-10).

Through this kind of prayerful reading, the gospels will come alive. It won't be enough to describe your insights simply as human wisdom or as the result of coincidence. You will sense the Holy Spirit moving in your heart and the wisdom of God filling your mind.

St. Ignatius and the Gospels
Before his conversion, Ignatius of Loyola used to imagine himself as a great warrior, a victorious hero, and a dashing knight whose

exploits won the heart of a fair princess. Ignatius had big dreams, and he set out to fulfill them by enlisting as a soldier in northern Spain.

However, Ignatius' dream was short-lived: He was wounded in battle and forced to remain in bed for months. During his convalescence, Ignatius began to read books about Jesus and the saints, and his imagination set to work again. This time, he began to imagine himself as a warrior for Jesus. He saw himself accomplishing great exploits for God. As Ignatius exercised his imagination in this way, the Holy Spirit lifted him up to a spiritual dimension and led him to give his life to Jesus.

From that point on, Ignatius' imagination played a vital role in his prayer life. He would imagine himself as an extra apostle at the Last Supper or at the raising of Lazarus from the dead or at the Transfiguration. In his mind's eye, Ignatius would imagine the setting, the time of day, the words that were spoken, and so much more—all with his natural mind. Then, he would imagine the kind of questions that he would ask Jesus and the answers Jesus would give him. Using his imagination, Ignatius would spend hours at a time pondering a scene from the gospels.

As Ignatius prayed in this way, the Holy Spirit lifted up his natural imagination to a spiritual level. He filled Ignatius with spiritual insight and spiritual wisdom and helped him to grasp the very mind of Christ (1 Corinthians 2:16). Ignatius taught this way of prayer—which he called his *Spiritual Exercises*—to anyone who came to him for guidance, and as a result, thousands of people came to meet Jesus through the gospels. Ignatius became convinced that this way of prayer was possible for anyone.

Experiencing Jesus in the Gospels

The gospels are meant to be studied on a historical and intellectual level, but they are also meant to be experienced on a spiritual level. If you set aside some time to study a gospel passage, you will undoubtedly see results. Your grasp of the gospels and their message will surely grow and develop. But if you go a step further and ask Jesus to lift your natural imagination up to the spiritual level, your life will be changed. You will experience the Holy Spirit working in you. You will want to love Jesus more. You will become both repentant and joyful. Your longing for the Eucharist will increase. You may even experience healing of past wounds and feel the weight of long-standing resentments being lifted off you.

Whenever you read the gospels, imagine yourself in the scene you are reading about and ask the Holy Spirit to lift you up. Expect that God will speak to you and draw you closer to himself. Trust that, with St. Ignatius, you will be moved to cry out:

> Take, Lord, and receive all my liberty, my memory, my intellect, and all my will—all that I have and possess. You gave it to me: to you, Lord, I return it! All is yours, dispose of it according to your will. Give me your love and grace, for this is enough for me. (*Spiritual Exercises*, 234)

Lamb of God

JOHN
1:1-51

John 1:1-18

¹ In the beginning was the Word, and the Word was with God, and the Word was God.

² He was in the beginning with God; ³ all things were made through him, and without him was not anything made that was made. ⁴ In him was life, and the life was the light of men. ⁵ The light shines in the darkness, and the darkness has not overcome it.

⁶ There was a man sent from God, whose name was John. ⁷ He came for testimony, to bear witness to the light, that all might believe through him. ⁸ He was not the light, but came to bear witness to the light. ⁹ The true light that enlightens every man was coming into the world. ¹⁰ He was in the world, and the world was made through him, yet the world knew him not. ¹¹ He came to his own home, and his own people received him not. ¹² But to all who received him, who believed in his name, he gave power to become children of God; ¹³ who were born, not of blood nor of the will of the flesh nor of the will of man, but of God.

¹⁴ And the Word became flesh and dwelt among us, full of grace and truth; we have beheld his glory, glory as of the only Son from the Father. ¹⁵ (John bore witness to him, and cried, "This was he of whom I said, 'He who comes after me ranks before me, for he was before me.' ") ¹⁶ And from his fullness have we all received, grace upon grace. ¹⁷ For the law was given through Moses; grace and truth came through Jesus Christ. ¹⁸ No one has ever seen God; the only Son, who is in the bosom of the Father, he has made him known.

In him was life, and the life was the light of men. (John 1:4)

John's Gospel begins not in Nazareth, Bethlehem, or Rome, but in the eternal glory of heaven. For John, salvation was not only a matter of Jesus' birth, death, and resurrection, but one of the eternal wisdom of Almighty God. That's why he wanted to make it clear from the very beginning that the eternal plan of God for our salvation was decisively advanced when the Word of God took on flesh and dwelt among us, full of grace and truth. These concepts boggle the mind, even as their beautiful telling in this gospel's prologue stir the heart. Do you know that it is God's desire to restore all people to his divine image? Do you know that Jesus took flesh and blood not just to free us from sin, but to make us into sons and daughters of God—members of the family of God and not just servants or disciples? Jesus took our old, fallen nature and put it to death on the cross so that we might be restored to the divine nature and become like Jesus.

Throughout his gospel, John will develop the themes that he sounds here in his prologue: light, life, truth, and glory. Each of these themes could take years of study and prayer to understand fully. In fact, we will not really know their depths until we are brought face to face with the Lord at the end of time. Yet John does not hesitate to bring them to our attention—not just because he wants us to contemplate their truth, but because he wants us to experience them in our lives on a day-to-day basis.

The life of Christ—the life given by the Holy Spirit—is our light. It is our hope and our joy day after day. The Son of God came to earth not just to teach us, but to transform us through his own grace and truth. Every day, we can meet Jesus in prayer, in the Eucharist, in our regular routines, and be lifted up to heaven. Every day, we can know a deeper share of the "grace upon grace" that God poured out in Christ (John 1:16)—and that grace can make us more like Jesus every day.

Jesus is constantly interceding for us in heaven. On earth, he continues to work out our sanctification through the Holy Spirit whom he has given us. Day in and day out, Jesus wants to reveal the Father to us and draw us into a closer relationship with him. He wants to transform our thoughts and actions. All he asks is that we keep our hearts open to him. As we do, we will know Jesus as our Savior, as our Friend, and as our Lord. We will receive another taste of the heavenly life that Jesus has come to give us.

"Jesus, you are the light of all men and women. Shine that light into my heart. May I know the power of your grace to transform me. Lord, I don't want just to be freed from sin. I want to become like you."

John 1:19-28

19   And this is the testimony of John, when the Jews sent priests and Levites from Jerusalem to ask him, "Who are you?" 20 He confessed, he did not deny, but confessed, "I am not the Christ." 21 And they asked him, "What then? Are you Elijah?" He said, "I am not." "Are you the prophet?" And he answered, "No." 22 They said to him then, "Who are you? Let us have an answer for those who sent us. What do you say about yourself?" 23 He said, "I am the voice of one crying in the wilderness, 'Make straight the way of the Lord,' as the prophet Isaiah said."

24   Now they had been sent from the Pharisees. 25 They asked him, "Then why are you baptizing, if you are neither the Christ, nor Elijah, nor the prophet?" 26 John answered them, "I baptize with water; but among you stands one whom you do not know, 27 even he who comes after me, the thong of whose sandal I am not worthy to untie." 28 This took place in Bethany beyond the Jordan, where John was baptizing.

John the Baptist was no ordinary man. He lived ascetically in the desert, wore camel skins, and ate locusts and wild honey. Crying out against injustice, he stirred souls to repentance and single-handedly caused a religious revival that touched even King Herod (Mark 6:17-20). While simple people hailed him as a prophet, the religious leaders deliberated. Who was this man? Was he Elijah, who was taken up to heaven and who would return to announce the Messiah (2 Kings 2:11; Malachi 4:5-6)? Was he the prophet foretold in Deuteronomy 18:18, who would come to speak the word of the Lord? Maybe he was the Messiah himself? John responded that he was none of these—only "the voice of one crying in the wilderness, 'Make straight the way of the Lord' " (John 1:23).

John told the people that he only baptized with water, but the one to give the Spirit was among them, even though they did not recognize him (John 1:26,33). Many Jews in John's time longed for the Messiah and yearned for the day when he would be revealed. But because their expectations were predefined, only a few recognized him when he did appear. Many were looking for a powerful king who would end Roman occupation and restore Israel to its former glory. Jesus, however, stood in their midst as the Lamb of God who would humbly submit to the cross for their sake.

When we look for God's action in our lives, what are we looking for? Do we limit the ways God can work. Do we "send" others to ask questions and discern God's movement, assuming that God would not answer our questions? Jesus has restored us to a personal relationship with God. Creator though he is, God wants to reveal himself to us in the quiet of prayer, in the words of scripture, and in the celebration of the Eucharist. He wants to speak to us through those around us and in the circumstances of our daily lives. Jesus is close to us. We need only set aside a little time each day to open our hearts to him and wait for him. When we do, we will hear him speak.

John 1:29-34

²⁹   The next day John saw Jesus coming toward him, and said, "Behold, the Lamb of God, who takes away the sin of the world! ³⁰ This is he of whom I said, 'After me comes a man who ranks before me, for he was before me.' ³¹ I myself did not know him; but for this I came baptizing with water, that he might be revealed to Israel." ³² And John bore witness, "I saw the Spirit descend as a dove from heaven, and it remained on him. ³³ I myself did not know him; but he who sent me to baptize with water said to me, 'He on whom you see the Spirit descend and remain, this is he who baptizes with the Holy Spirit.' ³⁴ And I have seen and have borne witness that this is the Son of God."

The long-awaited moment had finally come for John the Baptist! He had cried out in the wilderness, "Make straight the way of the Lord" (John 1:23). Now, he could declare, "Behold the Lamb of God, who takes away the sin of the world" (1:29). How his heart must have overflowed with joy and gratitude! His mission was completed as he testified to the Lamb of God—One whom he had not recognized before, but whom God had revealed to him at last: "I saw the Spirit descend as a dove from heaven, and it remained on him" (1:32).

Calling Jesus the Lamb of God, John fulfilled the scriptures that spoke of the Messiah as a lamb—gentle and humble, yet also strong and majestic. Jesus is the "lamb that is led to the slaughter" (Isaiah 53:7), yet he is also the one destined to lead the flock of God, delivering them from their foes, and ruling over them. We see this dual image most clearly in the Book of Revelation, where Jesus is depicted as the Lion of Judah who has conquered, and as the Lamb who alone is worthy to open the scroll of God's judgment (Revelation 5:5-14).

In his blessed moment of recognition, John was enabled to see Jesus as he never had before. Perhaps today holds similar blessed moments for us! Like John the Baptist, we too can receive divine revelation that will stir our hearts. The same Spirit who empowered Jesus and opened John's mind dwells within us. We received the Spirit at our baptism; he now waits for us to call upon him as our teacher and comforter. In prayer, ask the Spirit to reveal to you more about the Lamb of God who fulfills God's promises.

"Heavenly Father, thank you for sending your Son to give up his life so that I could know your love. By your Spirit, enlighten me to see Jesus' wonder and beauty as the mighty Lamb of God—slain, yet reigning in triumph as the King of kings."

John 1:35-42

³⁵ The next day again John was standing with two of his disciples; ³⁶ and he looked at Jesus as he walked, and said, "Behold, the Lamb of God!" ³⁷ The two disciples heard him say this, and they followed Jesus. ³⁸ Jesus turned, and saw them following, and said to them, "What do you seek?" And they said to him, "Rabbi" (which means Teacher), "where are you staying?" ³⁹ He said to them, "Come and see." They came and saw where he was staying; and they stayed with him that day, for it was about the tenth hour. ⁴⁰ One of the two who heard John speak, and followed him, was Andrew, Simon Peter's brother. ⁴¹ He first found his brother Simon, and said to him, "We have found the Messiah" (which means Christ). ⁴² He brought him

to Jesus. Jesus looked at him, and said, "So you are Simon the son of John? You shall be called Cephas" (which means Peter).   ❖

W hat does it mean to be a disciple? John's description of the calling of the first disciples can provide some help-ful insight.

When Jesus first called Andrew and his brother Simon, he did not tell them to go out and do great things, or that he would empower them to become great men. For their part, when Jesus asked them why they were following him, the disciples responded simply by asking if they could stay with him. They wanted to learn from Jesus and be with him. Jesus welcomed them, saying, "Come and see" (John 1:39). They spent the day with him, and he taught them.

Jesus' invitation to "come and see" extends to all of us in every age. We are all called to be his disciples, to come to Jesus and stay close to him. As we do, he will reveal himself to us and teach us, enabling us to be more like him. As a young boy, the Old Testament prophet Samuel learned this lesson, responding to the Lord's call with an open ear and open heart (1 Samuel 3-10).

How exciting it is that greatness in God's eyes relies not on what we do for God, but on what God does for us and in us! The disciples became great men of God because of the work of the Spirit within them. None of them was born with extraordinary intelligence or nobility of character. They were ordinary people who surrendered their lives to God and allowed the Holy Spirit to teach them, guide them, transform them, and empower them. As a result, they became humble vessels of God and were able to proclaim the gospel through-out the world. They delighted in pleasing God. Whether their words touched people's hearts or fell on deaf ears, they continued undaunted. Because they knew Jesus' love for them, pleasing God meant more to them than anything else in the world.

This is how deeply God wants us to know him. To God, it does not matter how smart we are or what we've accomplished. He calls us because he loves us. We are his special possessions, of greater value than anything else. He has chosen us to know him and to love him. Let us turn to the Lord humbly and open ourselves to receive from him.

John 1:43-51

⁴³ The next day Jesus decided to go to Galilee. And he found Philip and said to him, "Follow me." ⁴⁴ Now Philip was from Beth-saida, the city of Andrew and Peter. ⁴⁵ Philip found Nathana-el, and said to him, "We have found him of whom Moses in the law and also the prophets wrote, Jesus of Nazareth, the son of Joseph." ⁴⁶ Nathana-el said to him, "Can anything good come out of Nazareth?" Philip said to him, "Come and see." ⁴⁷ Jesus saw Nathana-el coming to him, and said of him, "Behold, an Israelite indeed, in whom is no guile!" ⁴⁸ Nathana-el said to him, "How do you know me?" Jesus answered him, "Before Philip called you, when you were under the fig tree, I saw you." ⁴⁹ Nathana-el answered him, "Rabbi, you are the Son of God! You are the King of Israel!" ⁵⁰ Jesus answered him, "Because I said to you, I saw you under the fig tree, do you believe? You shall see greater things than these." ⁵¹ And he said to him, "Truly, truly, I say to you, you will see heaven opened, and the angels of God ascending and descending upon the Son of man."

Nathanael is only mentioned in the Gospel of John, but many scholars believe he is the Bartholomew of the synoptic gospels, and thus one of the twelve apostles. As one of the pillars of the church, Nathanael's experience of Jesus is an important testimony to what it is like to encounter the Lord. His testimony tells us a great deal about what our own relationship with Jesus should be.

John tells us that Jesus first saw Nathanael sitting under a fig tree—an image popular with first-century rabbis of one who prayerfully pondered the law of the Lord. Jesus looked into Nathanael's heart and saw that he was a prayerful man. Consequently, he promised Nathanael a prayerful man's reward: a revelation of the opened heavens (John 1:51).

Today, Jesus looks into our hearts and offers us the same reward. He will open the gates of heaven to all who prayerfully seek him in scripture. He will reveal the mysteries of the kingdom of heaven to anyone who chooses to spend time with him in prayer. When we set aside time to pray and study God's word, we will be blessed, just as Nathanael was. God will reveal to us the truths of his kingdom. He will show us Jesus, the Son of God and the King of Israel. We will not just see these things intellectually. We will come to see them deep in our hearts, and the revelation will transform us.

Let us open our hearts to the revelation of Jesus, just as Nathanael did. As we do, a fire will begin to burn in us for our Savior. Our desire to know the Lord will burn ever more brightly, eventually consuming our whole lives. When we seek God humbly, we can be sure that he will transform our hearts and make them more and more pure. Let us take the time to consider the words of scripture and to pray fervently about them. As we draw closer to Jesus, we will be transformed, and heaven will be opened to us.

"Father, help me to pray and study God's word. Prepare my heart to understand your will. Make me pure as I seek your ways. Show me Jesus. Open heaven to the eyes of my heart so that I may see you in all your glory."

Author of New Life

JOHN
2:1-25

John 2:1-12

[1] On the third day there was a marriage at Cana in Galilee, and the mother of Jesus was there; [2] Jesus also was invited to the marriage, with his disciples. [3] When the wine failed, the mother of Jesus said to him, "They have no wine." [4] And Jesus said to her, "O woman, what have you to do with me? My hour has not yet come." [5] His mother said to the servants, "Do whatever he tells you." [6] Now six stone jars were standing there, for the Jewish rites of purification, each holding twenty or thirty gallons. [7] Jesus said to them, "Fill the jars with water." And they filled them up to the brim. [8] He said to them, "Now draw some out, and take it to the steward of the feast." So they took it. [9] When the steward of the feast tasted the water now become wine, and did not know where it came from (though the servants who had drawn the water knew), the steward of the feast called the bridegroom [10] and said to him, "Every man serves the good wine first; and when men have drunk freely, then the poor wine; but you have kept the good wine until now." [11] This, the first of his signs, Jesus did at Cana in Galilee, and manifested his glory; and his disciples believed in him.

[12] After this he went down to Caperna-um, with his mother and his brothers and his disciples; and there they stayed for a few days.

Jesus gave a puzzling reply to his mother in response to her request for help. He said, "My hour has not yet come" (John 2:4). Jesus spoke about this "hour" at other times and in other places as well (4:21; 12:27; 13:1; 17:1). For Jesus, this "hour" was the central reason why he had come into the world. It was the event toward which his whole existence was directed. Everything that Jesus said and did revolved around this "hour."

We were created so that we could be children of God and citizens of his kingdom. When we fell, God's purposes were not altered, even though Jesus had to come as Savior as well as Lord to retrieve us from bondage to Satan. The "hour" was the appointed time for the inauguration of the kingdom of God, the time when the will of God would be fulfilled. It was the time when Satan would be defeated and the forces of darkness overthrown.

This all-encompassing "hour" would divide all of history into "before" and "after" with Jesus at the center of God's plan for redemption. It would be the moment of our redemption, when the Father's beloved Son would take upon himself all the sins of the children of Adam. By shedding his blood, Jesus satisfied the justice and righteousness of God and reconciled us to the Father. Such was God's plan and God's will, a plan which Jesus embraced with all his heart.

We need to see this "hour" as not just a point in time but as our hour as well. Each individual must personally accept the hour that Jesus willingly endured for him or her. How can we do this? The answer is in Mary's words: "Do whatever he tells you" (John 2:5). Our salvation depends upon our living out of these words. Put your trust in Jesus. He will enable you to live in obedience to the Father's will.

"Eternal Father, I want to understand more fully how much you care for me. I believe that your plan of salvation for my life is fulfilled in the death and resurrection of your Son. Lord Jesus, I believe that your whole life was lived for the purposes of the hour of redemption.

Through the working of the Holy Spirit, I want this realization to penetrate the deepest part of me so I may live for love of you."

John 2:13-25

13   The Passover of the Jews was at hand, and Jesus went up to Jerusalem. 14 In the temple he found those who were selling oxen and sheep and pigeons, and the money-changers at their business. 15 And making a whip of cords, he drove them all, with the sheep and oxen, out of the temple; and he poured out the coins of the money-changers and overturned their tables. 16 And he told those who sold the pigeons, "Take these things away; you shall not make my Father's house a house of trade." 17 His disciples remembered that it was written, "Zeal for your house will consume me." 18 The Jews then said to him, "What sign have you to show us for doing this?" 19 Jesus answered them, "Destroy this temple, and in three days I will raise it up." 20 The Jews then said, "It has taken forty-six years to build this temple, and will you raise it up in three days?" 21 But he spoke of the temple of his body. 22 When therefore he was raised from the dead, his disciples remembered that he had said this; and they believed the scripture and the word which Jesus had spoken. 23   Now when he was in Jerusalem at the Passover feast, many believed in his name when they saw the signs which he did; 24 but Jesus did not trust himself to them, 25 because he knew all men and needed no one to bear witness of man; for he himself knew what was in man.

When we read the account of Jesus cleansing the temple, we can be distracted by what seems to be a fiery anger released against those who were using the temple for their own purposes. In fact, Jesus was performing a prophetic gesture in which he demonstrated his power and authority over the effects of spiritual darkness in our lives. Scripture reminds us that we are the "temple of the Holy Spirit" (1 Corinthians 6:19) and that we should "cleanse ourselves from every defilement of body and spirit" (2 Corinthians 7:1). In his death and resurrection, Jesus opened the way for our cleansing, and it is Jesus himself who personally accomplishes this in our lives—moment by moment—as we allow him into our hearts.

Throughout the Old Testament, we read about God drawing his people to himself and offering them a covenant with him which would manifest itself in obedience to his commandments. If we look at these laws as strict and confining, we can be discouraged. But if we look at them as the way into a free and happy life, we will be able to see the wisdom and love of God poured out in a very practical way.

Our God is a jealous God; he does not want anyone or anything to usurp the love and dedication that belong to him alone. Those of us who have experienced the love and devotion of a child know how wonderful it is, and how we don't want to lose it. However, we can see how easily children can get distracted, and how difficult it can be to keep their attention.

This gives us an idea of how we must appear to God. He cherishes our love, but he sees how we can be distracted by the lures of the world and by self-centered desires. God wants to open our minds to the true purpose of his commandments. They are meant to bring us joy and refreshment as we allow him to cleanse us and fill us more deeply with his love.

"Heavenly Father, come into my heart and free me from anything that distracts me from my commitment to you. I love you, Father; my life belongs to you. Give me the power to follow your commands and to serve you in gratitude and love."

The Promise of New Birth

JOHN
3:1-36

John 3:1-8

[1] Now there was a man of the Pharisees, named Nicodemus, a ruler of the Jews. [2] This man came to Jesus by night and said to him, "Rabbi, we know that you are a teacher come from God; for no one can do these signs that you do, unless God is with him." [3] Jesus answered him, "Truly, truly, I say to you, unless one is born anew, he cannot see the kingdom of God." [4] Nicodemus said to him, "How can a man be born when he is old? Can he enter a second time into his mother's womb and be born?"

[5] Jesus answered, "Truly, truly, I say to you, unless one is born of water and the Spirit, he cannot enter the kingdom of God. [6] That which is born of the flesh is flesh, and that which is born of the Spirit is spirit. [7] Do not marvel that I said to you, 'You must be born anew.' [8] The wind blows where it wills, and you hear the sound of it, but you do not know whence it comes or whither it goes; so it is with every one who is born of the Spirit."

Nicodemus, a wise and educated man, had heard Jesus' teaching, witnessed his miracles, and had come to reverence him deeply. But when Jesus told him that a second birth was necessary—so necessary that a person could not enter the kingdom of God without it—Nicodemus didn't understand.

The point that Nicodemus needed to learn is that those born of the Spirit are equipped with a new source of life, a share in the very life of God. Through the Spirit, they have a new relationship with God. They know him as a loving Father and are equipped with a new heart that is filled with the desires of God. They willingly turn their faces into the wind of the Spirit and allow that wind blow away everything in them that is not of him so that they can bear witness to God and give him glory.

St. Cyprian (who was martyred in 258 A.D.) spoke about the radical change that occurred in his own life when he was born anew:

> When the stain of my earlier life had been washed away by the help of the water of birth, and light from above had poured down upon my heart, now cleansed and purified; when I had drunk the Spirit of heaven and the second birth had restored me so to make me a new man; then straightway in a marvelous manner doubts began to be resolved, closed doors began to open, dark places to grow light; what before had seemed difficult was now easy, what I had thought impossible was now capable of accomplishment; so that I could now see that what had been born after the flesh and lived at the mercy of sin belonged to the earth while that which the Holy Spirit was enlivening had begun to belong to God. (*Treatise On the Grace of God*)

We have a loving Father who wants us to turn our faces into the wind of his Spirit and allow him to work in our lives. The same Spirit who transformed Cyprian wants to flow through us as well. His wind blows where it will. It brings salvation, new life, and the gifts necessary to unite and strengthen the body of Christ. It blows in our minds and hearts, teaching us to love, to raise families with the values of the kingdom of God, to seek humility and compassion in a world that emphasizes pride and self-seeking. Let us ask for the grace to live in a new way.

"Come, Holy Spirit, come! Continue the work you have begun in me!"

John 3:9-15

9 Nicodemus said to him, "How can this be?" 10 Jesus answered him, "Are you a teacher of Israel, and yet you do not understand this? 11 Truly, truly, I say to you, we speak of what we know, and bear witness to what we have seen; but you do not receive our testimony. 12 If I have told you earthly things and you do not believe, how can you believe if I tell you heavenly things? 13 No one has ascended into heaven but he who descended from heaven, the Son of man. 14 And as Moses lifted up the serpent in the wilderness, so must the Son of man be lifted up, 15 that whoever believes in him may have eternal life."

The Son of man must be lifted up. (John 3:14)

How easy it can be to overlook the importance of the cross of Jesus Christ. The message of the cross even seems incomprehensible to many. Still, the cross is at the heart of our Christian faith because through it, Jesus conquered the power of sin, Satan, and the world. By the power of his cross, we now share in the victory of his resurrection. Since the fall, all people had been under the dominion of the powers of darkness. With the triumph of the cross, however, these powers have been broken, and we can begin to live the resurrected life God wants for all his people.

The victory of the cross was so important that Jesus' entire life was directed toward it. It was prophesied of him, even from the days of his infancy (Luke 2:34-35), and as an adult, Jesus himself spoke of what was to come: "As Moses lifted up the serpent in the wilderness, so must the Son of man be lifted up, that whoever believes in him may have eternal life" (John 3:14-15; see also Matthew 17:22-23; Mark 9:30-31; Luke 9:43-44). Jesus recognized the need for atonement for sin and he held on to the promise that all people would be given new life through his obedience to the Father.

All those who have been baptized into Christ share in his victory. In faith, we can proclaim with Paul: "Our old self was crucified with him so that the sinful body might be destroyed, and we might no longer be enslaved to sin. . . . If we have died with Christ, we believe that we shall also live with him" (Romans 6:6-8). Jesus' triumph is our triumph. His cross is our salvation; it is our pledge of eternal life.

God our heavenly Father wants his people to have life, and life to the full (John 10:10). Let us remember the hopeful proclamation of the gospel: "God so loved the world that he gave his only Son, that whoever believes in him should not perish but have eternal life. For God sent the Son into the world, not to condemn the world, but that the world might be saved through him" (John 3:16-17). The triumph of the cross has brought us this life. Let us put our hope in it.

John 3:16-21

16 For God so loved the world that he gave his only Son, that whoever believes in him should not perish but have eternal life. 17 For God sent the Son into the world, not to condemn the world, but that the world might be saved through him. 18 He who believes in him is not condemned; he who does not believe is condemned already, because he has not believed in the name of the only Son of God. 19 And this is the judgment, that the light has come into the

world, and men loved darkness rather than light, because their deeds were evil. [20] For every one who does evil hates the light, and does not come to the light, lest his deeds should be exposed. [21] But he who does what is true comes to the light, that it may be clearly seen that his deeds have been wrought in God.

God so loved the world. (John 3:16)

If the entire meaning of human existence could be summed up in a single phrase, it would be this brief statement. God's love is the one constant in a world of shifting philosophies, politics, and fashions. It is the anchor that keeps humanity from drifting hopelessly off course. It is the magnetic center that keeps the world from spinning completely out of control. From the first spark of light to the universe's last breath, God's love remains unchanging, undiminished.

Scripture tells us that God created humanity out of love to be his special possession, a people who could take on the divine nature and love his Son as no other creature could. When we fell into sin, God continued to love us. He promised us a way out of the pain and division we had brought upon ourselves. In love, he spent generations preparing a people who could receive his salvation and proclaim it to the world. Centuries of war, hatred, poverty, and murder rolled by, and still God forgave and continued his intricate work of preparation.

When the time finally came, God showed the depth of his love. He sent his beloved Son into the world and gave him up as a sacrifice of atonement. Now anyone who believes in Jesus and is baptized in his name can be set free from sin and filled with the promised Holy Spirit. How deep the Father's love runs! How vast his compassion and mercy!

Faced with such love, we have a choice: Either to come into the light of God's love, or to remain in darkness. Coming into the light exposes our sins, but only so that we can be forgiven. Knowing God as a Father whose love never diminishes gives us the courage to open our hearts and trust him to pardon, not condemn. Those who cannot believe that God is so loving avoid the light and remain trapped in the guilt and condemnation of their sin.

The light of God's love is available to everyone. Let us come into that light more fully and allow him to scatter the darkness that lingers within us.

"Thank you, Father, for sending your Son to draw us back to you. As your children, we ask for a deeper experience of your love. Make us witnesses to this love to all the darkness that is still in the world."

John 3:22-30

²² After this Jesus and his disciples went into the land of Judea; there he remained with them and baptized. ²³ John also was baptizing at Aenon near Salim, because there was much water there; and people came and were baptized. ²⁴ For John had not yet been put in prison.

²⁵ Now a discussion arose between John's disciples and a Jew over purifying. ²⁶ And they came to John, and said to him, "Rabbi, he who was with you beyond the Jordan, to whom you bore witness, here he is, baptizing, and all are going to him." ²⁷ John answered,

"No one can receive anything except what is given him from heaven. [28] You yourselves bear me witness, that I said, I am not the Christ, but I have been sent before him. [29] He who has the bride is the bridegroom; the friend of the bridegroom, who stands and hears him, rejoices greatly at the bridegroom's voice; therefore this joy of mine is now full. [30] He must increase, but I must decrease."

A batter hits the winning run in a sports contest and is embraced by his joyful teammates. An executive completes an important business deal and sees the look of appreciation in the eyes of her boss and coworkers. A teenager graduates from high school and is photographed by proud parents. In our society, admiration generally comes only as a reward for some legitimate achievement or deed.

Yet John the Baptist revealed that Jesus looks at us differently. He rejoices in us simply for who we are, not for what we have accomplished or earned. We are the "bride" and Jesus is the bridegroom (Revelation 21:1-2). He looks at us with such joy that he sings and rejoices over us (Zephaniah 3:17). He delights in us as a lover delights in his beloved. He rejoices in doing good to us simply because he loves us (Jeremiah 32:40-41). Our "achievement" lies in accepting his love, and striving to live as his faithful bride.

As John observed Jesus beginning his work, he was happy to direct his followers to the "bridegroom." His motto became: "He must increase, but I must decrease" (John 3:30). The delight that John took in having a share in Jesus' love was greater than any satisfaction he might have felt in successfully performing the work given him. The mere sound of Jesus' voice caused John to rejoice (3:29).

Like John, we too can rejoice in our bridegroom as we await the final wedding feast (Revelation 19:9). It will be a time of rejoicing and celebration as pain, death, and mourning are destroyed and God wipes away every tear from our eyes (21:4). Just try to imagine the angels singing his praises joyfully as they see God's generous love for his bride. Try to imagine the gathering of all the redeemed from every age and every land, finally united with Jesus and one another in an unbreakable bond of love. Let these images fill your heart with joy and anticipation for that day.

As we go about our day, let us be assured that God rejoices and sings over us. Jesus, the bridegroom, longs to spend eternity with us!

"Jesus, thank you for loving me so much that you actually delight in me, even in my weaknesses. Lord, I want to be a part of your pleasing bride. Let your ways increase in me and my ways decrease. I thank you for making my joy full as I draw close to you."

John 3:31-36

[31] He who comes from above is above all; he who is of the earth belongs to the earth, and of the earth he speaks; he who comes from heaven is above all. [32] He bears witness to what he has seen and heard, yet no one receives his testimony; [33] he who receives his testimony sets his seal to this, that God is true. [34] For he whom God has sent utters the words of God, for it is not by measure that he gives the Spirit; [35] the Father loves the Son, and has given all things into his hand. [36] He who believes in the Son has eternal life; he who does not obey the Son shall not see life, but the wrath of God rests upon him.

L ight and darkness, belief and unbelief, above and below: John uses these words to convey what it means to turn from sin and live according to the ways of God. Jesus comes from above (John 3:31) and is the light sent by God (3:34). Our acceptance of Jesus as Savior leads us to the Father and brings us into the light of God's love. Turning away from Jesus leads to separation from God and leaves us abandoned to a life of darkness opposed to what God wants for his children. Yesterday, today, and tomorrow, choosing to live in darkness will evoke God's wrath.

What is God's wrath? It is often described in the Old Testament as divine anger at man's disobedience. The prophets used highly descriptive images, like a blazing, consuming fire, to convey God's wrath. Scripture gives us numerous examples of individuals, communities, even entire nations that were subjected to the wrath of God. But there is hope. Scripture always pairs God's wrath with his promise of mercy. God is completely devoted to his people. His wrath is tempered by his mercy because he longs to draw his children away from sin and back to himself.

Jesus' death on the cross is the supreme example of the interplay between wrath and mercy in the heart of God. Human disobedience had to be punished, yet we could never make full restitution for the way we dishonored God. So in his love, our Father sent his Son to pay the price we could never pay. God made the provision for everyone to be saved. Through the cross, the way was opened for the Holy Spirit to be given to us without measure (John 3:34), enabling us to obey God and experience fullness of life (3:36).

There will be a judgment when we will all be confronted by our sins. But we have this promise: "The LORD redeems the life of his servants; none of those who take refuge in him will be condemned" (Psalm 34:22). Let us place ourselves in God's hands and conform our lives to the gospel message of love and obedience. Every day, let us ask the Holy Spirit to be with us in all we do.

"Father, thank you for your mercy toward us. By sending Jesus, you have saved us. Send the light of the Holy Spirit to enlighten our hearts so that we can follow your loving ways and live each day in your victory."

Living Water

JOHN
4:1-54

John 4:1-15

[1] Now when the Lord knew that the Pharisees had heard that Jesus was making and baptizing more disciples than John [2] (although Jesus himself did not baptize, but only his disciples), [3] he left Judea and departed again to Galilee. [4] He had to pass through Samaria. [5] So he came to a city of Samaria, called Sychar, near the field that Jacob gave to his son Joseph. [6] Jacob's well was there, and so Jesus, wearied as he was with his journey, sat down beside the well. It was about the sixth hour.

[7] There came a woman of Samaria to draw water. Jesus said to her, "Give me a drink." [8] For his disciples had gone away into the city to buy food. [9] The Samaritan woman said to him, "How is it that you, a Jew, ask a drink of me, a woman of Samaria?" For Jews have no dealings with Samaritans. [10] Jesus answered her, "If you knew the gift of God, and who it is that is saying to you, 'Give me a drink,' you would have asked him, and he would have given you living water."

[11] The woman said to him, "Sir, you have nothing to draw with, and the well is deep; where do you get that living water? [12] Are you greater than our father Jacob, who gave us the well, and drank from it himself, and his sons, and his cattle?" [13] Jesus said to her, "Every one who drinks of this water will thirst again, [14] but whoever drinks of the water that I shall give him will never thirst; the water that I shall give him will become in him a spring of water welling up to eternal life." [15] The woman said to him, "Sir, give me this water, that I may not thirst, nor come here to draw." ▨▨▨

The light of God's truth can change the way in which we see our lives and the situations we encounter and have encountered. The story of the woman at the well is a striking example of how the Lord brought the light of truth to one lost in darkness.

Jesus met the woman of Samaria by Jacob's well. He could easily see her need—her inner thirst for forgiveness, acceptance, reconciliation, and hope. He knew that the woman's sinful life had darkened her mind and prevented her from grasping spiritual truths, and so he invited her to see her true condition and offered her "living water" (John 4:10). This was the Good Shepherd seeking out one who had strayed and offering to bring her back home.

While it was natural water that was on the woman's mind, Jesus was offering more than just the temporary relief and sustenance she was seeking at the well. He was offering eternal life, but the woman did not understand his meaning. As Jesus continued to reveal the nature of his living water, the woman again responded from the limits of her own human understanding. Once again, the compassion of the Son of God caused him to speak as he revealed the woman's spiritual darkness and her dire need for life.

We can hear in the woman's reply a longing to find God but an ignorance of where to look. How then was she to find God? Jesus showed her that the new life he could give would enable her to worship God in a new way. She would not be confined to any one time or place; as a child of God she would have access to the Father anywhere and at any time. Finally, Jesus, the fulfillment of the promise made to Abraham, Moses, and David, revealed himself to her as the Messiah for whom she was waiting. This was a moment of revelation, a moment of salvation for the fortunate woman!

How should we pray so that we too can receive the revelation of God—living water for our thirsty souls? We must humbly confess our sin and ask the Lord to forgive us and fill us "with the knowledge of his will in all spiritual wisdom and understanding" (Colossians 1:9). God is faithful. He will answer our prayers.

John 4:16-42

¹⁶ Jesus said to her, "Go, call your husband, and come here." ¹⁷ The woman answered him, "I have no husband." Jesus said to her, "You are right in saying, 'I have no husband'; ¹⁸ for you have had five husbands, and he whom you now have is not your husband; this you said truly." ¹⁹ The woman said to him, "Sir, I perceive that you are a prophet. ²⁰ Our fathers worshipped on this mountain; and you say that in Jerusalem is the place where men ought to worship." ²¹ Jesus said to her, "Woman, believe me, the hour is coming when neither on this mountain nor in Jerusalem will you worship the Father. ²² You worship what you do not know; we worship what we know, for salvation is from the Jews. ²³ But the hour is coming, and now is, when the true worshippers will worship the Father in spirit and truth, for such the Father seeks to worship him. ²⁴ God is spirit, and those who worship him must worship in spirit and truth." ²⁵ The woman said to him, "I know that the Messiah is coming (he who is called Christ); when he comes, he will show us all things." ²⁶ Jesus said to her, "I who speak to you am he." ²⁷ Just then his disciples came. They marveled that he was talking with a woman, but none said, "What do you wish?" or, "Why are you talking with her?" ²⁸ So the woman left her water jar, and went away into the city, and said to the people, ²⁹ "Come, see a man who told me all that I ever did. Can this be the Christ?" ³⁰ They went out of the city and were coming to him.

³¹ Meanwhile the disciples besought him, saying, "Rabbi, eat." ³² But he said to them, "I have food to eat of which you do not know." ³³ So the disciples said to one another, "Has any one brought him food?" ³⁴ Jesus said to them, "My food is to do the will of him who sent me, and to accomplish his work. ³⁵ Do you not say, 'There are yet four months, then comes the harvest? I tell you, lift up your eyes, and see how the fields are already white for harvest. ³⁶ He who reaps receives wages, and gathers fruit for eternal life, so that sower and reaper may rejoice together. ³⁷ For here the saying holds true, 'One sows and another reaps.' ³⁸ I sent you to reap that for which you did not labor; others have labored, and you have entered into their labor."

³⁹ Many Samaritans from that city believed in him because of the woman's testimony, "He told me all that I ever did." ⁴⁰ So when the Samaritans came to him, they asked him to stay with them; and he stayed there two days. ⁴¹ And many more believed because of his word. ⁴² They said to the woman, "It is no longer because of your words that we believe, for we have heard for ourselves, and we know that this is indeed the Savior of the world."

Wells and watering places have a singularly important meaning among people living in arid regions. After a drought, water miraculously restores life to a desert-like earth and revives humans, animals, and plants alike, rescuing them from death. For this reason, the Old Testament prophets and sages often spoke of living water to signify the gifts that would flow when the Messiah finally came (Zechariah 14:8; Ezekiel 47:8-10).

We can imagine that when Jesus came upon Jacob's well he recalled the scriptural tradition that the Messiah would be the source of a kind of water that would sustain a person's life eternally. As the promised Messiah, Jesus' mission was to do the Father's will and "to accomplish his work" (John 4:34), and the "work" that the Father had given him was to give eternal life to all people (17:2). This must have occupied Jesus' thoughts as the Samaritan woman approached the well.

As we read about this encounter, we see the patience and love Jesus had as he brought the woman to believe in him as the source of living water. At first she took him for a normal Jew (John 4:9), then she realized that he was a learned person, perhaps a rabbi, and began to refer to him as "Sir" (4:11). Then she understood him to be a prophet (4:19). At last she sensed that he may well be the promised Messiah as he claimed (4:25).

The woman had come to the well to fetch water for the day ahead. After meeting Jesus, however, she left her water jar behind. She now had within her a spring of water that would last forever. She went back into the town to herald Jesus as the Messiah (John 4:29,39-42). Many in the town also received living water as they in turn encountered Jesus and came to believe in him themselves.

As believers, we can ask the Holy Spirit to awaken an appreciation for the "gift of God" in our hearts (John 4:10). The wells of our souls do need to be cleansed of all things earthly that prevent us from encountering Christ in the routine of our lives—but this is something that Jesus loves to do for every one of us. As we reflect on the truths of God proclaimed in Jesus' encounter with the Samaritan woman, let us allow those waters to spring up within us once again.

John 4:43-54

[43] After the two days he departed to Galilee. [44] For Jesus himself testified that a prophet has no honor in his own country. [45] So when he came to Galilee, the Galileans welcomed him, having seen all that he had done in Jerusalem at the feast, for they too had gone to the feast.

[46] So he came again to Cana in Galilee, where he had made the water wine. And at Caperna-um there was an official whose son was ill. [47] When he heard that Jesus had come from Judea to Galilee, he went and begged him to come down and heal his son, for he was at the point of death. [48] Jesus therefore said to him, "Unless you see signs and wonders you will not believe." [49] The official said to him, "Sir, come down before my child dies." [50] Jesus said to him, "Go; your son will live." The man believed the word that Jesus spoke to him and went his way. [51] As he was going down, his servants met him and told him that his son was living. [52] So he asked them the hour when he began to mend, and they said to him, "Yesterday at the seventh hour the fever left him." [53] The father knew that was the hour when Jesus had said to him, "Your son will live"; and he himself believed, and all his household. [54] This was now the second sign that Jesus did when he had come from Judea to Galilee.

The official from Capernaum faced difficult questions. Could this simple carpenter from Nazareth be the Messiah? And, if so, did he really possess the divine power to heal? He chose to believe in Jesus, and his need drove him to travel twenty miles to Cana and beg Jesus to heal his son. Surprisingly, Jesus rebuked him, saying, "Unless you see signs and wonders you will not believe" (John

4:48). Through this harsh statement—which was directed to the people as well as to the official—Jesus was calling for a faith that is "the assurance of things hoped for, the conviction of things not seen" (Hebrews 11:1).

Crises demand decisions that demonstrate whether we have faith. Do we trust in God's promises, power, and love? Do we believe that he uses all circumstances for the good of those who love him (Romans 8:28)? Or do we rely on human intelligence, our limited perspective, and our own small ability to control events? When we choose to believe in God, we open ourselves to his peace, even in the most disturbing circumstances. If we rely only on human reasoning, we risk failure and, along with it, discouragement, frustration, and fear.

When our faith is challenged, many of us find ourselves echoing the words of the apostle Thomas, "Unless I see . . . I will not believe" (John 20:25). Jesus knows our inclination toward unbelief and self-reliance. That's why he died for us. If we confess our unbelief to him and ask for his help, he will empower us with the gift of living faith. Then, as we grow closer to him through the sacraments, prayer, and scripture, we will develop childlike trust. His promises of justification, forgiveness, reconciliation with neighbors, and eternal union with God will come alive for us.

As we recognize the futility of unaided human effort in overcoming temptation and sin, we will learn to cleave to the promises of God fulfilled through Christ. We will discover, as did Abraham when he was asked to sacrifice his long-awaited son, that God will provide (Genesis 22:1-18). No matter what happens, God always deserves our trust.

"Heavenly Father, you are my provider and protector. You gave up your beloved Son for me so that all your promises would become a reality in my life. I love you and entrust my life to you."

Jesus, Healer and Judge

JOHN
5:1-47

John 5:1-16

[1] After this there was a feast of the Jews, and Jesus went up to Jerusalem.

[2] Now there is in Jerusalem by the Sheep Gate a pool, in Hebrew called Beth-zatha, which has five porticoes. [3] In these lay a multitude of invalids, blind, lame, paralyzed. [5] One man was there, who had been ill for thirty-eight years. [6] When Jesus saw him and knew that he had been lying there a long time, he said to him, "Do you want to be healed?" [7] The sick man answered him, "Sir, I have no man to put me into the pool when the water is troubled, and while I am going another steps down before me." [8] Jesus said to him, "Rise, take up your pallet, and walk." [9] And at once the man was healed, and he took up his pallet and walked.

Now that day was the sabbath. [10] So the Jews said to the man who was cured, "It is the sabbath, it is not lawful for you to carry your pallet." [11] But he answered them, "The man who healed me said to me, 'Take up your pallet, and walk.' " [12] They asked him, "Who is the man who said to you, 'Take up your pallet, and walk'?" [13] Now the man who had been healed did not know who it was, for Jesus had withdrawn, as there was a crowd in the place. [14] Afterward, Jesus found him in the temple, and said to him, "See, you are well! Sin no more, that nothing worse befall you." [15] The man went away and told the Jews that it was Jesus who had healed him. [16] And this was why the Jews persecuted Jesus, because he did this on the sabbath.

John's Gospel progresses through a stream of "witnesses"—people and events—all pointing to the truth of Jesus' identity. Among these are the many powerful signs Jesus performed, like healing the lame man by the pool of Bethzatha.

What is most striking about this miracle is what Jesus did not do. He neither touched the man or washed him in the pool. He only spoke the words: "Rise, take up your pallet, and walk" (John 5:8), and the man was healed. This healing pointed dramatically to a central truth about Jesus as the Son of God: His very word is power.

Other parts of John's narrative demonstrate the power of Christ's word. For instance, at a wedding feast in Cana, Jesus only had to speak a word of command, and water was turned into wine (John 2:7-11). He healed a royal official's son simply through his word (4:50-53). And near the end of the gospel, before surrendering to his adversaries, Jesus flattened them with a word of truth (18:6). Jesus possessed such power because he is the Logos—the Word of God through whom everything was created (1:1-3). He is the Word made flesh (1:14) through whom we are redeemed: "Truly, truly, I say to you, he who hears my word and believes him who sent me, has eternal life; he does not come into judgment, but has passed from death to life" (5:24).

No wonder Mary said, "Do whatever he tells you" (John 2:5). She knew the power of Jesus' word to transform lives. Many others, including many of the religious leaders, did not. Even the man who was healed "went away and told the Jews" (5:15). He had the opportunity to stay with Jesus and allow his words to penetrate his heart, but he left too soon.

Day after day, God calls us to be renewed by his word of life through the liturgy, in prayer and by reading scripture. As we quiet ourselves in God's presence, we can come to hear his word more clearly. It will become "living and active" in our hearts (Hebrews 4:12). And we will be changed.

"Lord, help me to walk always with you. I want to be made whole again. Teach me never to doubt that your word has power. I cry out to you in faith: 'Lord, I am not worthy to receive you, but only say the word, and I will be healed.' "

John 5:17-30

[17] But Jesus answered them, "My Father is working still, and I am working." [18] This was why the Jews sought all the more to kill him, because he not only broke the sabbath but also called God his Father, making himself equal with God. [19] Jesus said to them, "Truly, truly, I say to you, the Son can do nothing of his own accord, but only what he sees the Father doing; for whatever he does, that the Son does likewise. [20] For the Father loves the Son, and shows him all that he himself is doing; and greater works than these will he show him, that you may marvel. [21] For as the Father raises the dead and gives them life, so also the Son gives life to whom he will. [22] The Father judges no one, but has given all judgment to the Son, [23] that all may honor the Son, even as they honor the Father. He who does not honor the Son does not honor the Father who sent him. [24] Truly, truly, I say to you, he who hears my word and believes him who sent me, has eternal life; he does not come into judgment, but has passed from death to life. [25] "Truly, truly, I say to you, the hour is coming, and now is, when the dead will hear the voice of the Son of God, and those who hear will live. [26] For as the Father has life in himself, so he has granted the Son also to have life in himself, [27] and has given him authority to execute judgment, because he is the Son of man. [28] Do not marvel at this; for the hour is coming when all who are in the

tombs will hear his voice [29] and come forth, those who have done good, to the resurrection of life, and those who have done evil, to the resurrection of judgment.

[30] "I can do nothing on my own authority; as I hear, I judge; and my judgment is just, because I seek not my own will but the will of him who sent me."

What was the source of Jesus' power? What was the secret of his ability to heal people of their physical, emotional, and spiritual wounds? The obvious answer, of course, is that he could perform those miracles because he is the Son of God. Yet scripture shows us that it wasn't only because of who Jesus was. It was also because of how he lived. Jesus' relationship with his Father was so deep, his reliance on his Father was so complete, that he did nothing except what he saw his Father doing (John 5:19).

Throughout his ministry, Jesus spoke of his Father as the source of his power. He spoke of being "in" the Father, just as the Father is "in" him (John 10:38). He addressed him as *Abba*, an Aramaic word meaning Dad or "Papa" (Mark 14:36). He spoke of his desire to do only what his Father wanted of him (John 6:38) and to speak only the words the Father gave him (8:28). Jesus' life was one of constant prayer to his Father (Luke 6:12; Matthew 14:23) as he allowed the Holy Spirit to lead him and empower him (Matthew 4:1; Luke 4:18).

What does all this mean for us? It means that, when we look at Jesus, we see God the Father himself. When we see Jesus' mercy, compassion, self-sacrifice, and love, we are witnessing a perfect portrayal of God. What a corrective this is to our view of God as a wrathful judge or distant observer!

Let us come to our heavenly Father in prayer each day, confident of his love for us. Let us humble ourselves and confess how totally dependent we are upon him. He wants to hold us in his arms and fill us with his Holy Spirit. Through Jesus, we can experience an intimacy with God our loving Father that surpasses anything we can imagine. Like Jesus, we can be empowered to bring the Father's love and healing to others. We too will do the works of Jesus, and even greater works, and so bring glory to our loving, heavenly Father (John 14:12,13,21; 17:26).

"Father, you are merciful and compassionate. I hear you calling me to an intimate relationship with you. I put my trust in your love and I give you my heart and my will. May I know your love in a deeper way, and share your love with others."

John 5:31-36

[31] "If I bear witness to myself, my testimony is not true; [32] there is another who bears witness to me, and I know that the testimony which he bears to me is true. [33] You sent to John, and he has borne witness to the truth. [34] Not that the testimony which I receive is from man; but I say this that you may be saved. [35] He was a burning and shining lamp, and you were willing to rejoice for a while in his light. [36] But the testimony which I have is greater than that of John; for the works which the Father has granted me to accomplish, these very works which I am doing, bear me witness that the Father has sent me."

How many of us, when we read the words that John the Baptist "has borne witness to the truth" (John 5:33), sort of skip over it and just assume that it's pretty self-evident what it means? But, what is truth, after all? Is it trustworthiness? Honesty? Conformity with reality? Agreement with a standard rule?

In the Bible, the concept of truth rests not on our mental processes but on the faith experience of a personal encounter with God. John the Baptist acknowledged this when he said, "I myself did not know him [Jesus]; but he who sent me to baptize with water said to me, 'He on whom you see the Spirit descend and remain, this is he who baptizes with the Holy Spirit.' And I have seen and have borne witness that this is the Son of God" (John 1:33-34). The truth that John testified to, therefore, is the truth of the gospel—the revealed Word of the Father, fulfilled in Jesus Christ, and made known to us by the Holy Spirit, which we must receive in faith so that our lives can be changed. If we expect to arrive at the truth solely by our intellectual abilities, we are likely to be disappointed.

Have you ever noticed, for example, how the logic of the world can seem more believable and acceptable to our fallen minds than the truth of God? In fact, the world's values often seek to turn the gospel upside down. In human terms, it makes no sense that the Son of God would be born in a stable rather than a palace, or that he would first be revealed to ignorant shepherds rather than to the theologians or political leaders of his day. It is folly that he should later die on a cross rather than conquer the world with an army of angels. Even in your own family, there are perhaps some who rebel at the proclamation of the truth of the gospel and who would rather follow their natural inclinations than the truth of God.

Yet, like John, we are called to testify to the truth. We cannot do it by our own intellectual skill, but we do have the Holy Spirit who comes into our minds and hearts and convinces us that Jesus is Lord and that anyone can receive him into their hearts. Just as John bore witness to the truth not just through his words, but through his life, let us commit ourselves to living according to the truth. Let us ask the Holy Spirit to reveal more and more of that truth to us as we seek the Lord in prayer.

"Holy Spirit, convince me of the truth of who Jesus is, so that I may proclaim it to family and friends and testify to this truth in the way I lead my life."

John 5:37-47

37 "And the Father who sent me has himself borne witness to me. His voice you have never heard, his form you have never seen; 38 and you do not have his word abiding in you, for you do not believe him whom he has sent. 39 You search the scriptures, because you think that in them you have eternal life; and it is they that bear witness to me; 40 yet you refuse to come to me that you may have life. 41 I do not receive glory from men. 42 But I know that you have not the love of God within you. 43 I have come in my Father's name, and you do not receive me; if another comes in his own name, him you will receive. 44 How can you believe, who receive glory from one another and do not seek the glory that comes from the only God? 45 Do not think that I shall accuse you to the Father; it is Moses who accuses you, on whom you set your hope. 46 If you believed Moses, you would believe me, for he wrote of me. 47 But if you do not believe his writings, how will you believe my words?"

You search the scriptures. . . yet you refuse to come to me. (John 5:39,40)

How do you view the church? Theologically accurate doctrines? A rich, venerable tradition? Solid moral teaching? Moving liturgies and rituals? All of these are vital elements of the church, yet, if we place any of them above the person of Jesus, we will not experience God's life within us. None of these elements have any meaning if they are separated from their connection to Jesus, the head of the church and the one for whom and through whom everything was made (Colossians 1:16,18).

The same principle applies to scripture. If we do not allow the Spirit to write the word of God on our hearts, then scripture is all too easily reduced to historical information and intriguing stories. St. Paul even warned that, apart from its God-given purpose, scripture can become an instrument of death, for "the written code kills, but the Spirit gives life" (2 Corinthians 3:6).

Adhering to scripture—without being open to the Spirit—was the problem that Jesus met in many of the religious leaders of his day. They knew the Hebrew Bible better than most people, yet they failed to see that it pointed to Jesus. Thus, they missed the life that God was offering them through his Son.

We may ask how they failed to see Jesus for who he was. Yet the same power of sin that can cause us not to recognize Jesus had the same effect on them. Human pride, self-righteousness, and hardness of heart can dull anyone to the Lord. It's possible for anyone to retain information about Jesus and still lose a living connection with him. We may even try to live according to the principles that Jesus taught and still not come to him for life. This only leaves us striving for perfection by our own strength—an effort that all too often ends in frustration and discouragement.

Jesus is calling us to come to him to receive the life that scripture speaks about and that the church upholds so beautifully. In prayer, let us turn to Jesus for the divine life he offers. Let us ask to experience his mercy so that we can put aside self-righteousness and harshness toward others and become merciful as he is.

"Lord Jesus, I turn to you for life. I have no source of love apart from you. Fill me with yourself, so that your love may flow through me to other people."

Bread of Life

JOHN
6:1-71

John 6:1-15

[1] After this Jesus went to the other side of the Sea of Galilee, which is the Sea of Tiberi-as. [2] And a multitude followed him, because they saw the signs which he did on those who were diseased. [3] Jesus went up on the mountain, and there sat down with his disciples. [4] Now the Passover, the feast of the Jews, was at hand. [5] Lifting up his eyes, then, and seeing that a multitude was coming to him, Jesus said to Philip, "How are we to buy bread, so that these people may eat?" [6] This he said to test him, for he himself knew what he would do. [7] Philip answered him, "Two hundred denarii would not buy enough bread for each of them to get a little." [8] One of his disciples, Andrew, Simon Peter's brother, said to him, [9] "There is a lad here who has five barley loaves and two fish; but what are they among so many?" [10] Jesus said, "Make the people sit down." Now there was much grass in the place; so the men sat down, in number about five thousand. [11] Jesus then took the loaves, and when he had given thanks, he distributed them to those who were seated; so also the fish, as much as they wanted. [12] And when they had eaten their fill, he told his disciples, "Gather up the fragments left over, that nothing may be lost." [13] So they gathered them up and filled twelve baskets with fragments from the five barley loaves, left by those who had eaten. [14] When the people saw the sign which he had done, they said, "This is indeed the prophet who is to come into the world!" [15] Perceiving then that they were about to come and take him by force to make him king, Jesus withdrew again to the mountain by himself. ▨▨▨

The sixth chapter of the Gospel of John focuses on Jesus as the bread of life and can be divided into four basic sections: 1) the multiplication of the loaves (6:1-15); 2) Jesus walking on the water (6:16-21); 3) his discourse, telling his followers that he is the bread of life (6:22-59); and 4) positive and negative reactions to Jesus' teaching (6:60-71).

This story of Jesus feeding the multitude is the only miracle found in all four gospels—a point which highlights its importance for the church. No matter where we find the miracle recounted, one of the most striking elements of the story is the people's hunger and Jesus' readiness to feed them. In John's Gospel, however, the focus is first on the people's hunger to hear Jesus' words and to see him—the reason why Jesus seems always to be surrounded by a "large crowd" (6:2). The people were attracted to Jesus because they sensed that he offered them something they needed to make their lives complete.

John tells us that the people who followed Jesus up the mountain were physically hungry—and this was the hunger that Jesus met first. In recounting this miracle story, John places Jesus in the forefront of the action. It is Jesus who saw the people's need and took the initiative to feed them (compare with Matthew 14:15-16; Luke 9:12-13). He saw their physical need and began a conversation with Philip that would result in a miraculous feeding and his teaching on the bread of life. As he prepared to offer the few loaves to the people, Jesus first "gave thanks" (*eucharisto* in Greek) over them (John 6:11). And then, he proceeded to feed them with more than enough to satisfy their hunger.

Both physically and spiritually, Jesus cared for his people, even those who would reject him (6:66). Because he didn't want anyone to perish, he constantly offered them his love and healing. Jesus knows our hunger and is able to satisfy our every need. Are you hungry? Do you feel empty inside? Do you feel confused or hurt? Turn to Jesus, the Bread of Life, and allow him to feed you.

"Jesus, you are the Bread of Life, given for the life of the world. Come fill us with your peace and love. In word and sacrament, satisfy our hunger and heal all our hurts."

John 6:16-21

16 When evening came, his disciples went down to the sea, 17 got
into a boat, and started across the sea to Caperna-um. It was now
dark, and Jesus had not yet come to them. 18 The sea rose because
a strong wind was blowing. 19 When they had rowed about three or
four miles, they saw Jesus walking on the sea and drawing near to
the boat. They were frightened, 20 but he said to them, "It is I; do
not be afraid." 21 Then they were glad to take him into the boat,
and immediately the boat was at the land to which they were
going.

The people were so impressed by Jesus' multiplication of the loaves and fishes that they wanted to make him king and set him up in opposition to the traitor Herod. But Jesus would not accept such a move because it would provoke Roman military intervention. More importantly, to be crowned a temporal king would have represented a complete misinterpretation of the kingdom that Jesus had come to establish. As he would state emphatically before Pilate, his kingdom was not of this world (John 18:36). So, Jesus hid himself on the mountain, and his disciples took to the sea in order to avoid any adverse consequences.

But the disciples' troubles didn't end once they had escaped the crowd. Throughout scripture, "the sea" is considered a place of chaos, the dwelling place of evil spirits and dangerous forces over which God must exert powerful restraint (Psalm 18:16-17; Isaiah 17:12-13). Fleeing the pressures of the crowd, the disciples found themselves confronted by powers they could neither escape or control. Understandably, they were frightened.

At this point of crisis, when all human resources had been expended, Jesus appeared, walking on the water. This man, who could multiply loaves and fish, demonstrated a still greater power when he took decisive authority over the violent sea. When he spoke, his words were not merely comforting—"Do not be afraid" (John 6:20). He also declared, "I am he"—a phrase which his disciples would have recognized as a title belonging only to Yahweh, the one true God (Exodus 3:14; John 8:58).

In this story, Jesus manifested the power of God—a power that encompasses both control over evil forces and safety and protection for those whom he has called. Once he brought his disciples safe to dry ground, Jesus went on to speak about the need for all people to participate in his life—to the extent of actually eating his body and drinking his blood. But before we begin to examine these powerful truths, we have a chance to rest on the side of the lake and to ponder the greatness and compassion of our God.

"Lord Jesus, I believe that you are the holy God, sovereign in power and perfect in love. By your grace, help me to place my faith and trust in you. May I be open to your great love and mercy; and may my heart become as still in your presence as you made the waters."

John 6:22-29

²² On the next day the people who remained on the other side of the sea saw that there had been only one boat there, and that Jesus had not entered the boat with his disciples, but that his disciples had gone away alone. ²³ However, boats from Tiberi-as came near the place where they ate the bread after the Lord had given thanks. ²⁴ So when the people saw that Jesus was not there, nor his disciples, they themselves got into the boats and went to Caperna-um, seeking Jesus.

²⁵ When they found him on the other side of the sea, they said to him, "Rabbi, when did you come here?" ²⁶ Jesus answered them, "Truly, truly, I say to you, you seek me, not because you saw signs, but because you ate your fill of the loaves. ²⁷ Do not labor for the food which perishes, but for the food which endures to eternal life, which the Son of man will give to you; for on him has God the Father set his seal." ²⁸ Then they said to him, "What must we do, to be doing the works of God?" ²⁹ Jesus answered them, "This is the work of God, that you believe in him whom he has sent."

This is the work of God, that you believe in him whom he has sent.
(John 6:29)

This statement probably surprised the crowd that had followed Jesus to the other side of the lake. They sought him out because they were amazed by his multiplication of the loaves and fishes, and they were puzzled by how he had crossed the lake without a boat. Jesus reprimanded them for seeking him only as a miracle worker who could satisfy their material needs and make their lives more comfortable and interesting. They failed to see him as one sent from God.

How easy it is for us to make that same mistake—looking to Jesus only to satisfy our personal needs and make our lives more pleasant. Jesus says the same thing to us that he said to the crowd: "Believe in him whom he has sent" (John 6:29). This is what it means to do the work of God.

The word used for "work" in this passage is the Greek word, *ergon*, a word that denotes hard labor and physical exertion. It's easy to think that belief in Jesus is an easy matter, something that requires only emotional or intellectual assent. In fact, to believe in Jesus as Savior, we are called to deny our desire for independence and self-sufficiency and submit our lives to Jesus instead. It means that we must turn from sin and embrace Jesus' commands and his will over and above our own. This is work!

On a practical level, what does this work entail? How are we to do the work of believing in the Son of God? Prayer, reading scripture, and serving one another must become top priorities for us because through them, we dispose ourselves to the transforming presence of the Spirit. It is true that we are changed by the power of God and not by human effort alone. But the work that we must do is the work of bringing our hearts (which can so love independence and self-reliance) before the throne of God so that we can be changed. Jesus is the Son of God. He is worthy of our lives. Let us work to bring ourselves before him. Let us ask, seek, and knock, so that he will fill us with his life.

"Holy Spirit, help me to understand what it means to do the work of God. Father, grant that I would be willing to work to come into the presence of Jesus and to believe that he is well worth my time and effort."

John 6:30-35

³⁰ So they said to him, "Then what sign do you do, that we may see, and believe you? What work do you perform? ³¹ Our fathers ate the manna in the wilderness; as it is written, 'He gave them bread from heaven to eat.' " ³² Jesus then said to them, "Truly, truly, I say to you, it was not Moses who gave you the bread from heaven; my Father gives you the true bread from heaven. ³³ For the bread of God is that which comes down from heaven, and gives life to the world." ³⁴ They said to him, "Lord, give us this bread always."

³⁵ Jesus said to them, "I am the bread of life; he who comes to me shall not hunger, and he who believes in me shall never thirst."

The similarity between the miracle of the manna (Exodus 16:4) and the multiplied bread and fish (John 6:1-13) was not lost on the people who pursued Jesus across the Sea of Galilee. Still, we may be amazed that after so great a miracle, and after Jesus' exhortation to believe in him (6:29), the crowd still asked to see another sign (6:30).

Rather than work another wonder, Jesus continued to speak to them so that he could show them more clearly how unique he was and how worthy of their faith and trust he was. He began by telling them that he was the fulfillment of all that Moses did and stood for: "It was not Moses who gave you the bread from heaven; my Father gives you the true bread from heaven" (John 6:32). The change from the past tense, *gave*, to the present, *gives*, is significant. The bread of the past—the manna in the desert—satisfied the Israelites' physical needs and sustained them for their journey to the promised land. Now the new bread—the only Son of God—is in their midst, and he has promised so much more than manna. He has come to satisfy every hunger the human heart could ever know.

Like Moses, Jesus was sent by God to lead his people from slavery into the promised land of freedom. Yet Jesus is greater than Moses. Moses gave the people a food that perished every night, and he led them to an earthly promised land. Jesus, however, gives himself as the bread of eternal life. He leads his people out slavery to sin and into the kingdom of heaven, the land of all God's promises. In the past we were only partially satisfied; now we can be fully satisfied as we come to Jesus and receive his body and blood.

This is how generous Jesus is! He never fails to offer us his very life, the living bread that comes down from heaven. No other food is as sweet, as fulfilling, as this bread. Everything else—as good and pleasant as it may be—pales in comparison, simply because this gift from God is everlasting and is meant just for us. Nothing else can so fill our needs.

"Jesus, I believe that you are the Bread of Life, the only one who can satisfy my deepest hunger. I join with the whole church as I pray, 'Lord, give us this bread always.' "

John 6:36-40

36 "But I said to you that you have seen me and yet do not believe. 37 All that the Father gives me will come to me; and him who comes to me I will not cast out. 38 For I have come down from heaven, not to do my own will, but the will of him who sent me; 39 and this is the will of him who sent me, that I should lose nothing of all that he has given me, but raise it up at the last day. 40 For this is the will of my Father, that every one who sees the Son and believes in him should have eternal life; and I will raise him up at the last day."

Having drawn the right questions out of the crowd, Jesus began to tell them that he is the bread of life who satisfies every human hunger. How can we understand these words?

One place to start is in scripture itself. It is not uncommon for the Old Testament to speak about God's word and wisdom as a kind of "bread" that gives life to God's people (Proverbs 9:1-6; Sirach 24:1-2,19-22). In the Lord's Prayer, which Jesus taught his disciples, the phrase "our daily bread" is used to sum up all the gifts which are necessary for our well being and our relationship with God (Matthew 6:11). Finally, at the Last Supper, Jesus chose bread as the sign and instrument of the greatest of gifts—his life in the Eucharist (Luke 22:19-20).

Jesus told the people that he himself is the gift that his heavenly Father gives to his people. Since this gift imparts the abundant and everlasting life of heaven, those who come to Jesus will never hunger again, because they will lack nothing. Jesus Christ, the Bread of Life, is sufficient for all our needs and can bring life where only death seems to reign.

To come to Jesus is to believe that God sent him to save us from sin and give us fullness of life. God wants us to know that this is his work, and it is his work alone. We cannot come to Jesus unless the Father draws us—unless the Father stirs us to hope in his mercy and love (John 6:44). Jesus also promised that he will not lose anyone whom the Father gives him. No, he will raise them up to new life (6:39).

Because Jesus is the Bread of Life, and because he will never reject anyone who comes to him, we can approach him confidently with all of our cares, our sins, our hurts, and our fears. If he can satisfy the desire to be freed from death that is in every human heart, how much more is he able and willing to care for all the needs that we face in this life as well?

"Lord Jesus, you are the Bread of Life, the advocate who ever lives to intercede for us. We are secure and safe in you. We come to you today to receive your life. Fill us up, Lord, and make us ready to greet you when you come again."

John 6:41-51

41 The Jews then murmured at him, because he said, "I am the bread which came down from heaven." 42 They said, "Is not this Jesus, the son of Joseph, whose father and mother we know? How does he now say, 'I have come down from heaven'?" 43 Jesus answered them, "Do not murmur among yourselves. 44 No one can come to me unless the Father who sent me draws him; and I will

raise him up at the last day. ⁴⁵ It is written in the prophets, 'And they shall all be taught by God.' Every one who has heard and learned from the Father comes to me. ⁴⁶ Not that any one has seen the Father except him who is from God; he has seen the Father. ⁴⁷ Truly, truly, I say to you, he who believes has eternal life. ⁴⁸ I am the bread of life. ⁴⁹ Your fathers ate the manna in the wilderness, and they died. ⁵⁰ This is the bread which comes down from heaven, that a man may eat of it and not die. ⁵¹ I am the living bread which came down from heaven; if any one eats of this bread, he will live for ever; and the bread which I shall give for the life of the world is my flesh."

What a great miracle the manna in the desert was to the starving Israelites (Exodus 16)! It was one of the great miracles of the Exodus to which faithful Jews clung for centuries. It consoled them in times of trial that God would never abandon them, and in times of plenty it reminded them that every good gift comes from God. Even so, those who ate of the gift of manna eventually died. Was God limited in his ability to provide for his people?

Jesus promised food that would bring eternal life. That food was his flesh. He said: "I am the living bread which came down from heaven; if anyone eats of this bread, he will live forever; and the bread which I shall give for the life of the world is my flesh" (John 6:51). Jesus would give the fulfillment of the promise foreshadowed in the manna. He would give himself as the living bread to be our sustenance forever.

In his farewell discourse at the Last Supper, Jesus promised his disciples: "I will not leave you desolate; I will come to you" (John

14:18). Picking up on this theme, Pope John Paul II, in his encyclical *On the Holy Spirit*, said:

> The most complete sacramental expression of the "departure" of Christ through the mystery of the Cross and Resurrection is the Eucharist. In every celebration of the Eucharist, his coming, his salvific presence, is sacramentally realized: in the Sacrifice and in Communion. It is accomplished by the power of the Holy Spirit, as part of his own mission. (62)

The Eucharist is the point of meeting between the word of God, the cross, and the power of the Holy Spirit. On the cross, Jesus gave his flesh for the life of the world. In the fullest sense, the cross is the total event of the word of God. In the Eucharist, he gives us his flesh to eat. The action of eating implies the absorbing and assimilating into one's person the revelation of Jesus Christ. This becomes the basis of one's whole life.

The Eucharist has always been a foundational part of Christian life. Luke wrote that the brethren "devoted themselves to . . . the breaking of bread and the prayers" (Acts 2:42). Our partaking of the Eucharist cannot be a passive affair. We must know and acknowledge Jesus whom we are receiving. Then, in him we will have life and have it abundantly (John 10:10).

"Father, thank you for Jesus, the Bread of Life. Thank you that the Spirit is always with me to bring me closer to Jesus. I believe that he is the ultimate source of my strength, hope, and consolation."

John 6:52-59

52 The Jews then disputed among themselves, saying, "How can this man give us his flesh to eat?" 53 So Jesus said to them, "Truly, truly, I say to you, unless you eat the flesh of the Son of man and drink his blood, you have no life in you; 54 he who eats my flesh and drinks my blood has eternal life, and I will raise him up at the last day. 55 For my flesh is food indeed, and my blood is drink indeed. 56 He who eats my flesh and drinks my blood abides in me, and I in him. 57 As the living Father sent me, and I live because of the Father, so he who eats me will live because of me. 58 This is the bread which came down from heaven, not such as the fathers ate and died; he who eats this bread will live for ever." 59 This he said in the synagogue, as he taught at Caperna-um.

As Jesus taught the people about the bread of life, he told them that he himself was the life-giving bread sent from the Father. In this final portion of his teaching, he challenged those who came to him: "The bread which I shall give for the life of the world is my flesh" (John 6:51). In response to the Jews' disputes over these words, Jesus simply repeated: "Unless you eat the flesh of the Son of man and drink his blood, you have no life in you; he who eats my flesh and drinks my blood has eternal life" (6:53-54).

To John's original readers, the constant litany—"eat," "drink," "flesh," "blood"—would have resonated with the same sacramental overtones that they hold for us, turning their thoughts toward the Eucharist. In the sacrament of the Eucharist, we are connected with the one atoning sacrifice by which Jesus offered himself "for the life of the world" (6:51).

Every time we celebrate this mystery, that same sacrifice is somehow made present to us. According to the *Catechism of the Catholic Church*, the Eucharist is a "memorial" in the biblical sense of the word: "not merely the recollection of past events but the proclamation of the mighty works wrought by God for men. In the liturgical celebration of these events, they become in a certain way present and real" (CCC, 1363).

The Eucharist is not just a reminder; it is a real sacrifice and a real gift. "In the Eucharist, Christ gives us the very body which he gave up for us on the cross" (CCC, 1365). Whenever we celebrate the Mass, we participate in a representation of Jesus' death and resurrection. When we receive Jesus with a disposition of faith and love, we enter into those actual events of his life-giving sacrifice. We not only receive bread and wine—or flesh and blood, for that matter. We receive salvation. Let us rejoice that Jesus has given this gift to all generations until he returns in glory.

"Lord Jesus, thank you for your sacrifice on the cross and your resurrection to new life. Thank you for making that redemption present whenever we celebrate the Eucharist. We humbly accept your presence among us, and we trust in your great promise that whoever eats your body and drinks your blood abides in you."

John 6:60-71

[60] Many of his disciples, when they heard it, said, "This is a hard saying; who can listen to it?" [61] But Jesus, knowing in himself that his disciples murmured at it, said to them, "Do you take offense at this? [62] Then what if you were to see the Son of man ascending where he was before? [63] It is the spirit that gives life, the flesh is of no avail;

the words that I have spoken to you are spirit and life. [64] But there are some of you that do not believe." For Jesus knew from the first who those were that did not believe, and who it was that would betray him. [65] And he said, "This is why I told you that no one can come to me unless it is granted him by the Father."

[66] After this many of his disciples drew back and no longer went about with him. [67] Jesus said to the twelve, "Do you also wish to go away?" [68] Simon Peter answered him, "Lord, to whom shall we go? You have the words of eternal life; [69] and we have believed, and have come to know, that you are the Holy One of God." [70] Jesus answered them, "Did I not choose you, the twelve, and one of you is a devil?" [71] He spoke of Judas the son of Simon Iscariot, for he, one of the twelve, was to betray him.

The words that I have spoken to you are spirit and life. (John 6:63)

Jesus had just delivered a central teaching to the people concerning the gift of his body and blood as a source of life to all Christians. The reality of this truth must be as much a part of our spiritual lives as food and drink are to our physical lives. Yet, even Jesus' own disciples found the teaching hard to understand, and even harder to accept.

John tells us that some of those who listened to Jesus turned away at this point and followed him no longer (John 6:66). As a consequence, they received nothing more from him. However, those whose minds were open to God were able to receive the promise of eternal life, even though their understanding of his words remained incomplete. This contrast between those who left and those who remained illustrates an important spiritual truth: A mind dominated by the flesh insists upon understanding before it will believe. However, the spiritual mind will believe even before it has full understanding.

If we try to grasp the truths of God's kingdom with our human minds alone, we will conclude that the gospel is foolishness (1 Corinthians 1:18). In order to understand what pleases God, we must call upon his Holy Spirit for enlightenment—in prayer, in scripture, and by seeking his will throughout the day. Often we believe that if we had more education, greater intelligence, or deeper understanding, we would be more able to please God, be "better Christians," and live his word more readily. But we must recall Jesus' words: "It is the spirit that gives life, the flesh is of no avail" (John 6:63).

To think according to God's mind, we must ask the Spirit to teach us. God said: "As the heavens are higher than the earth, so are my ways higher than your ways and my thoughts than your thoughts" (Isaiah 55:9). All our human resources were affected by our fall into sin and are therefore unable to bring us into a personal, living knowledge of the Father. It is only by the Holy Spirit that spiritual truths can come to life for us and bring us into a new relationship with God. Let us ask the Spirit to enlighten our minds and give us greater understanding about the truths of our faith.

Controversies
and Arguments

JOHN
7:1–8:59

John 7:1-13

¹ After this Jesus went about in Galilee; he would not go about in Judea, because the Jews sought to kill him. ² Now the Jews' feast of Tabernacles was at hand. ³ So his brothers said to him, "Leave here and go to Judea, that your disciples may see the works you are doing. ⁴ For no man works in secret if he seeks to be known openly. If you do these things, show yourself to the world." ⁵ For even his brothers did not believe in him. ⁶ Jesus said to them, "My time has not yet come, but your time is always here. ⁷ The world cannot hate you, but it hates me because I testify of it that its works are evil. ⁸ Go to the feast yourselves; I am not going up to this feast, for my time has not yet fully come." ⁹ So saying, he remained in Galilee.

¹⁰ But after his brothers had gone up to the feast, then he also went up, not publicly but in private. ¹¹ The Jews were looking for him at the feast, and saying, "Where is he?" ¹² And there was much muttering about him among the people. While some said, "He is a good man," others said, "No, he is leading the people astray." ¹³ Yet for fear of the Jews no one spoke openly of him.

Anyone who thought he had Jesus figured out was doomed to frustration. Just when a person thought he knew Jesus well enough to predict what he would do, Jesus would do something different. Jesus would preach against sin, but dine with sinners. He would heal hundreds of sick people (Luke 6:17-19), but then refuse at first to speak to someone who requested healing (Matthew 15:22-23). He would travel to village after village in order to alert people to the coming of God's kingdom (Mark 1:38); yet when he had the opportunity to attend a festival in Jerusalem where he could address huge crowds of people, he said he would not go (John 7:6-9).

Even when Jesus did what people expected, often it was not for the reasons they would have thought. After refusing to go to the festival in Jerusalem, Jesus did go (John 7:10), but not in order to achieve celebrity status, as his relatives hoped, but to make himself known as the one who offers men and women life with God (compare John 7:3-4 with 7:37-39 and 8:12).

Jesus was unpredictable not because he was whimsical or capricious, but because he followed the leading of the Holy Spirit. He always acted in a way that expressed his Father's love for those he encountered. He surprised people because he was perfectly in harmony with God's plan, and God's plan can be very surprising to earthbound human beings.

People should find us, as Jesus' followers, somewhat unpredictable as well (see John 3:8). Unfortunately, however, we often want to have everything mapped out and provided for in advance. We get a sense of security from knowing what to expect. But Jesus challenges us to believe that God's plans exceed our expectations. Perhaps the reason some people have not been won over to Jesus is because they have not yet experienced the unexpected gift of his love through us, his followers. If we were more attentive to the leading of the Spirit, quicker to move in obedience to his urging, perhaps more people would be touched by God's great love.

Perhaps God has something new in store for us today. We will never know, unless we are sensitive to the Spirit. Let's not box him in!

"Holy Spirit, I am willing to follow your guidance, even if it leads me into something unfamiliar and uncomfortable. Help me remain open to you. Let me find my security in your love, not in my established routines."

John 7:14-24

[14] About the middle of the feast Jesus went up into the temple and taught. [15] The Jews marveled at it, saying, "How is it that this man has learning, when he has never studied?" [16] So Jesus answered them, "My teaching is not mine, but his who sent me; [17] if any man's will is to do his will, he shall know whether the teaching is from God or whether I am speaking on my own authority. [18] He who speaks on his own authority seeks his own glory; but he who seeks the glory of him who sent him is true, and in him there is no falsehood. [19] Did not Moses give you the law? Yet none of you keeps the law. Why do you seek to kill me?" [20] The people answered, "You have a demon! Who is seeking to kill you?" [21] Jesus answered them, "I did one deed, and you all marvel at it. [22] Moses gave you circumcision (not that it is from Moses, but from the fathers), and you circumcise a man upon the sabbath. [23] If on the sabbath a man receives circumcision, so that the law of Moses may not be broken, are you angry with me because on the sabbath I made a man's whole body well? [24] Do not judge by appearances, but judge with right judgment."

Jesus healed a man who had been unable to walk for thirty-eight years (John 5:1-18), but instead of honoring this miracle-worker, the religious leaders were angry at him. The healing took place on the sabbath, and to their minds, this broke Jewish law. Jesus warned them against being misled by appearances rather than using good judgment (7:24). If it is acceptable to circumcise an infant on the sabbath to make him physically "whole" as a member of Israel, how could it not be acceptable to heal a man's whole body on the sabbath? (7:23). Jesus understood that these people were not truly concerned for God's will, and that this was why they found him so difficult to understand or accept (7:17).

The problem of judging from appearances is familiar to all of us. The world tells us to do whatever feels good; to look to successful and fashionable people as role models; to be more concerned with keeping up appearances than with justice and mercy. The devil loves it when we take a superficial view because it makes it easier for him to distract us from Jesus.

Sometimes we face tricky situations, in which it is difficult to determine what is right or most useful to do. It isn't possible for us always to make the best decisions. We are, after all, only on the road to perfection; we haven't arrived yet. But Jesus put his finger on the one question that we need to ask: Am I trying to do God's will? If our heart is in the right place, we will be much more open to God's guidance—humble and teachable in the presence of the Spirit.

The popular slogan among young Christians—What would Jesus do?—states the issue well. It reminds us that Jesus wants to raise our minds to think with him. It urges us to set aside our desires and ask God for his wisdom.

How can we obtain godly wisdom? Reading scripture helps build a kind of "database" of insights to rely on. Prayer to the Holy Spirit opens us to a deeper knowledge of God and his ways. It is helpful to bounce our thoughts off a brother or sister in Christ whom we can trust, to see if they line up with the gospel. We will make mistakes, because we are in a learning process. We should not get discouraged. If we are willing, God will continue to teach us.

"Lord Jesus, I give you my mind and heart today. Work freely in my life. Make me aware of your thoughts for each situation I am in today. Give me the grace to desire what you desire."

John 7:25-36

²⁵ Some of the people of Jerusalem therefore said, "Is not this the man whom they seek to kill? ²⁶ And here he is, speaking openly, and they say nothing to him! Can it be that the authorities really know that this is the Christ? ²⁷ Yet we know where this man comes from; and when the Christ appears, no one will know where he comes from." ²⁸ So Jesus proclaimed, as he taught in the temple, "You know me, and you know where I come from? But I have not come of my own accord; he who sent me is true, and him you do not know. ²⁹ I know him, for I come from him, and he sent me." ³⁰ So they sought to arrest him; but no one laid hands on him, because his hour had not yet come. ³¹ Yet many of the people believed in him; they said, "When the Christ appears, will he do more signs than this man has done?"

³² The Pharisees heard the crowd thus muttering about him, and the chief priests and Pharisees sent officers to arrest him. ³³ Jesus then said, "I shall be with you a little longer, and then I go to him who sent me; ³⁴ you will seek me and you will not find me; where I am you cannot come." ³⁵ The Jews said to one another, "Where does this man intend to go that we shall not find him? Does he intend to go to the Dispersion among the Greeks and teach the Greeks? ³⁶ What does he mean by saying, 'You will seek me and you will not find me,' and, 'Where I am you cannot come'?"

The Jewish Feast of Booths (or Tabernacles) was an annual feast of thanksgiving for the fall harvest. At this feast, the people recalled the pillar of fire that led their ancestors through the desert (Exodus 40:36-38) and the time when Moses brought water out of a rock (Numbers 20:11). It is not inappropriate, then, that during this feast Jesus would tell the people that he had come to provide streams of living water (John 7:37-38) and proclaim himself as the light of the world (8:12).

Some of the Jews who heard Jesus preaching in the temple were perplexed over this man whom some considered to be the promised Messiah: "We know where this man is from; but when the Messiah comes, no one will know where he is from" (John 7:27). They knew he came from Nazareth, so could he really be the Messiah? Yet, did they really know his origin? It is one thing to say that he is a Galilean (7:52), but it is another thing altogether to understand that he came from God the Father, full of grace and truth (1:14).

The confusion about Jesus' divine and human origins points to one of the primary distinctions vital for all of us—the difference between flesh and spirit. In "the flesh," that is, relying solely on our human reason and senses, we can know quite a lot about Jesus: his ancestry, his movements, and maybe even why his friends liked him and his enemies hated him. But it is only in "the spirit"—by the Spirit of God—that we can learn truths about Jesus that can change our lives. This type of knowledge—spiritual knowledge that transforms—comes to us as we sit humbly with the scriptures and ask the Spirit to speak his words of truth to our hearts. It is in these times of prayer and meditation that we learn about Jesus' true origins and that we begin to desire to be with him where he is.

Jesus promised his disciples that the Spirit would remind them of everything he taught while he was with them (John 14:26). Let us seek this same Spirit and ask that Jesus' words be written on our hearts.

"Holy Spirit, come into my heart today and transform me. Raise me above the ways of the flesh so that I can see Jesus and embrace him in love and humility."

John 7:37-39

³⁷ On the last day of the feast, the great day, Jesus stood up and proclaimed, "If any one thirst, let him come to me and drink. ³⁸ He who believes in me, as the scripture has said, 'Out of his heart shall flow rivers of living water.' " ³⁹ Now this he said about the Spirit, which those who believed in him were to receive; for as yet the Spirit had not been given, because Jesus was not yet glorified.

There is no certain "place" we can go to find the fullness of life for which we thirst. In order to receive it, we must come to a "person"—Jesus Christ. Nothing else will satisfy, bring everlasting joy, or give us hope. Only in Christ and through the outpouring of the Holy Spirit do we begin to experience a spiritual life where we hunger and thirst no more, where we are sheltered and satisfied by God, and where every tear is wiped away (Revelation 7:15-17). The Holy Spirit is the Spirit of power, the life and love who makes available to us the riches of God.

Through belief in Christ Jesus, we can experience more fully this outpouring of the Spirit in our own lives. Jesus said: "He who believes in me, as the scripture has said, 'Out of his heart shall flow rivers of living water' " (John 7:38). Belief in Jesus and in God's provision for his people's salvation (1:12; 3:16-21,36) opens us to life through the work of the Spirit in us.

It is important that we accept that belief in Jesus is more than just intellectual or theoretical knowledge. It is a willingness to abandon our reservations and fears and to base our lives on Jesus. When we say we believe, we assert our confidence in God rather than in ourselves. Every time we exercise this belief that we confess, we open ourselves to the glory and power of Christ to work in our lives through his Holy Spirit.

The gift of the Holy Spirit is more than God's personal gift to us for our own good; it is the outpouring of God's love upon all of creation. The Spirit is like a mighty river that flows out into the land from the city of God (Ezekiel 47:1-12; Revelation 22:1-5). It is poured into people's hearts in order to bring life to all the world. This great stream issues forth to bring life to places that cannot and do not know life otherwise.

Everywhere the Spirit goes, new life springs up as people are nourished and healed. Through the indwelling Holy Spirit, every believer becomes a member in the body of Christ. By the power of the Spirit, we can all receive the full, perfect, and eternal life that God has promised his children. Rejoice today in God's gift of life for you—his gift of love, his gift of power. Rejoice in the outpouring of the Holy Spirit and pray that its flow would be increased and deepened in your heart and all over the world.

John 7:40-53

40 When they heard these words, some of the people said, "This is really the prophet." 41 Others said, "This is the Christ." But some said, "Is the Christ to come from Galilee? 42 Has not the scripture said that the Christ is descended from David, and comes from Bethlehem, the village where David was?" 43 So there was a division among the people over him. 44 Some of them wanted to arrest him, but no one laid hands on him.

45 The officers then went back to the chief priests and Pharisees, who said to them, "Why did you not bring him?" 46 The officers

answered, "No man ever spoke like this man!" [47] The Pharisees answered them, "Are you led astray, you also? [48] Have any of the authorities or of the Pharisees believed in him? [49] But this crowd, who do not know the law, are accursed." [50] Nicodemus, who had gone to him before, and who was one of them, said to them, [51] "Does our law judge a man without first giving him a hearing and learning what he does?" [52] They replied, "Are you from Galilee too? Search and you will see that no prophet is to rise from Galilee." [53] They went each to his own house.

Military personnel are trained to obey orders without question. It's meant to be a reflex action; pausing to think about the wisdom of an order could cost many lives. This ancient principle is still carried on today in armies the world over. What, then, happened to the temple guards? The chief priests had long objected to the outlandish claims and disruptive healings of Jesus. Now that he was attracting crowds in the temple, it was time to make their displeasure clear: they dispatched the temple guards to arrest him.

Imagine the chief priests' surprise when the guards came back empty-handed! Maybe it isn't so surprising, though. While military protocol is a powerful thing, even more powerful is the attractiveness of Jesus. The temple guards were simple, ordinary men who actually listened to Jesus. They were often foreigners, less swayed by the surrounding politics, and certainly not among Jerusalem's sophisticated caste. They all had needs and wounds and desires for God's love—perhaps like many soldiers today. When they heard Jesus speak, something touched their hearts.

Those who didn't accept Jesus supported their positions

with half-truths and bad intellectual arguments. One argument was that Jesus couldn't be the Messiah because he healed on the sabbath. Yet no one questioned why priests were allowed to circumcise on the sabbath. Another objection was that Jesus couldn't be the Messiah because the Messiah was to come from Bethlehem, and Jesus came from Nazareth. But he was, in fact, born in Bethlehem, the city of Joseph's ancestor David.

God wants us to come to him with simplicity and an honest understanding of our needs. He wants us to approach him with humble, quiet minds. Preconceived notions of who Jesus is cannot erase the truth of his claims and the persistence of his call. God wants our hearts, which are crying out for his touch. Let us put aside the temptation to make God fit into our limited categories. Let us instead open our hearts to his word.

"Father, thank you for sending Jesus so that I could see, hear, and love him. May his words be like a magnet to my heart, drawing me closer to heaven. Help me put down my guard and listen to him in love."

John 8:1-11

[1] But Jesus went to the Mount of Olives. [2] Early in the morning he came again to the temple; all the people came to him, and he sat down and taught them. [3] The scribes and the Pharisees brought a woman who had been caught in adultery, and placing her in the midst [4] they said to him, "Teacher, this woman has been caught in the act of adultery. [5] Now in the law Moses commanded us to stone such. What do you say about her?" [6] This they said to test him,

that they might have some charge to bring against him. Jesus bent down and wrote with his finger on the ground. [7] And as they continued to ask him, he stood up and said to them, "Let him who is without sin among you be the first to throw a stone at her." [8] And once more he bent down and wrote with his finger on the ground. [9] But when they heard it, they went away, one by one, beginning with the eldest, and Jesus was left alone with the woman standing before him. [10] Jesus looked up and said to her, "Woman, where are they? Has no one condemned you?" [11] She said, "No one, Lord." And Jesus said, "Neither do I condemn you; go, and do not sin again."

The scribes and the Pharisees, looking for a chance to trap Jesus, thought they had found a situation that would serve their purposes perfectly. They had Jesus caught between the demands of Mosaic law and the law of the occupying Roman forces. If Jesus, in response to their question, was "soft" and pardoned the woman caught in adultery, how could he claim to be faithful to the tradition of Moses? On the other hand, if he advocated stoning her to death, he would be liable to prosecution by the Romans, who had taken away from the Jews the right to put anyone to death. There was no way they could lose in this situation.

What the Pharisees did not take into account were Jesus' deep love and compassion for humanity. They did not understand his claim that "God did not send the Son into the world to condemn the world, but in order that the world might be saved through him" (John 3:17). Jesus knew that every person in the world had been deeply tainted by sin; that everyone, regardless of outward appearances, was in slavery to sin and desperately needed the salvation he came to offer.

Jesus' words to the woman caught in adultery—"Go, and do not sin again" (John 8:11)—should encourage us. Our desire is often to avoid sin, but we sometimes feel powerless in rejecting temptation and overcoming sinful patterns. To know that Jesus believes us capable of overcoming sin (through him, of course) should give us great encouragement. He knows our hearts, but he also knows his transforming power.

Paul's words to the Philippians can give us hope in this regard as well: "Indeed I count everything as loss because of the surpassing worth of knowing Christ Jesus my Lord" (Philippians 3:8); "I want to know Christ and the power of his resurrection" (3:10); "I press on toward the goal for the prize of the upward call of God in Christ Jesus" (3:14). Paul's words express a heart set on Jesus, a heart that knows Jesus intimately and personally. They reflect one who has had a true conversion and who desires to turn from sin and embrace Jesus and the life he offers. When these qualities are reflected in our hearts, we too will be strengthened in our attempts to overcome sin by the power of God in us.

Let us open our hearts to Jesus so that we might know him more intimately, love him more fully, and follow him more faithfully. We will find that the same power that freed Jesus from the grave will strengthen and free us from our sinful patterns and enable us to walk faithfully with him.

John 8:12-20

[12] Again Jesus spoke to them, saying, "I am the light of the world; he who follows me will not walk in darkness, but will have the light of life." [13] The Pharisees then said to him, "You are bearing witness to yourself; your testimony is not true." [14] Jesus answered, "Even if I do bear witness to myself, my testimony is true, for I know whence I have come and whither I am going, but you do not know whence I come or whither I am going. [15] You judge according to the flesh, I judge no one. [16] Yet even if I do judge, my judgment is true, for it is not I alone that judge, but I and he who sent me. [17] In your law it is written that the testimony of two men is true; [18] I bear witness to myself, and the Father who sent me bears witness to me." [19] They said to him therefore, "Where is your Father?" Jesus answered, "You know neither me nor my Father; if you knew me, you would know my Father also." [20] These words he spoke in the treasury, as he taught in the temple; but no one arrested him, because his hour had not yet come.

I am the light of the world. (John 8:12)

This was quite an extraordinary claim that Jesus made. Essentially, he was announcing that he had the power to overcome all the darkness of evil that any man or woman who followed him would ever face. It was a staggeringly new concept for his hearers to digest. They believed that following the law of Moses would bring them release from evil. Now Jesus was telling them that they needed to follow not a law but a person, Jesus himself, in order to have "the light of life." No wonder they found Jesus hard to accept!

The law of Moses required at least two witnesses (two "testimonies") in a trial (Deuteronomy 19:15). Consequently, some Pharisees called Jesus' words into question: He hadn't produced witnesses who could testify to the claims he was making about himself. But who actually could testify? Only Jesus himself, who was the Son of God, and his Father, who had sent him (John 8:18).

When Jesus mentioned his Father, the religious leaders immediately asked where his Father was. Jesus replied, "You know neither me nor my Father. If you knew me, you would know my Father also" (John 8:19). This statement revealed the main problem: Though they were scrupulous observers of the law, these Pharisees had not related to God on a heartfelt, personal level. Because they did not know him, they did not recognize his Son.

The exchange between Jesus and the Pharisees can lead us to ask whether we know Jesus and, through him, the Father. Is Jesus the light of our lives? Are we open to his light? We are all tempted to wall off parts of our lives from his light—to let his light shine in one area, such as Sunday worship, while closing off the rest of our week from his radiance. If we do that, we protect ourselves for a while from having to face any surprises, yet we also run the risk of missing out on all that God can do in our lives.

Through the indwelling Holy Spirit, God is with us every moment of the day. The mighty God who has redeemed us wants to break the chains that bind us—chains of sin, fear, anxiety, illness, and emotional pain. His dazzling light will cast out the darkness wherever it shines. Let us open our hearts to him.

"Jesus, I want my life to reflect your light. Shine your light in every corner of my life. Fill me with your joy, so that others may see your light and give glory to God."

John 8:21-30

21 Again he said to them, "I go away, and you will seek me and die in your sin; where I am going, you cannot come." 22 Then said the Jews, "Will he kill himself, since he says, 'Where I am going, you cannot come'?" 23 He said to them, "You are from below, I am from above; you are of this world, I am not of this world. 24 I told you that you would die in your sins, for you will die in your sins unless you believe that I am he." 25 They said to him, "Who are you?" Jesus said to them, "Even what I have told you from the beginning. 26 I have much to say about you and much to judge; but he who sent me is true, and I declare to the world what I have heard from him." 27 They did not understand that he spoke to them of the Father. 28 So Jesus said, "When you have lifted up the Son of man, then you will know that I am he, and that I do nothing on my own authority but speak thus as the Father taught me. 29 And he who sent me is with me; he has not left me alone, for I always do what is pleasing to him." 30 As he spoke thus, many believed in him.

Jesus told his opponents that he is the unique revelation of the Father, because he is the Son of God, perfectly aligned with the Father's will (John 8:28-29). Jesus did nothing without the Father; he could say only what the Father "taught" him. To the religious leaders who had trouble accepting this, Jesus said that to disbelieve in his oneness with the Father meant that they would die in their sins (8:24). Fortunately, many of Jesus' listeners did come to believe in him (8:30).

Jesus' message is very clear. Faith that he is the Son of God leads to life. Disbelief leads to death. Our tendency might be to look down on those Pharisees who refused to believe in Jesus. Instead, their lack of belief should spur us to examine our own faith. Is our faith in Christ limited to an intellectual agreement with Christian doctrine, an assent that we express in a dutiful, perhaps mechanical way? Do we recite prayers simply as formulas, or as expressions of love and trust in Jesus? Do we open our hearts every day to the power of the Holy Spirit? Faith is a tremendous gift from God. Do we receive it and exercise it on a daily basis?

The first place we are called to exercise our faith is in prayer. Experiment with your prayer life. Ask God to teach you how to worship him and how to detect the movements of the Holy Spirit in your heart. When you read scripture, try to put aside other distractions and trust that God wants to speak to you through his word. Make specific prayers of intercession for others, trusting that with even a small amount of faith, you can move mountains.

No matter where you are in your prayer life, there is always room for more. Jesus wants to give you greater faith and a deeper experience of his love. In prayer, allow his love to break through in your heart! Speak to him sincerely and honestly. Believe that if you ask him for greater faith, he will give it.

"Father, I praise you for the love you have revealed in Jesus. I worship you with my whole heart. Grant me a greater faith in your Son so that I may know your presence more fully."

John 8:31-42

31 Jesus then said to the Jews who had believed in him, "If you continue in my word, you are truly my disciples, 32 and you will know the truth, and the truth will make you free." 33 They answered him, "We are descendants of Abraham, and have never been in bondage to any one. How is it that you say, 'You will be made free'?"

34 Jesus answered them, "Truly, truly, I say to you, every one who commits sin is a slave to sin. 35 The slave does not continue in the house for ever; the son continues for ever. 36 So if the Son makes you free, you will be free indeed. 37 I know that you are descendants of Abraham; yet you seek to kill me, because my word finds no place in you. 38 I speak of what I have seen with my Father, and you do what you have heard from your father."

39 They answered him, "Abraham is our father." Jesus said to them, "If you were Abraham's children, you would do what Abraham did, 40 but now you seek to kill me, a man who has told you the truth which I heard from God; this is not what Abraham did. 41 You do what your father did." They said to him, "We were not born of fornication; we have one Father, even God." 42 Jesus said to them, "If God were your Father, you would love me, for I proceeded and came forth from God; I came not of my own accord, but he sent me."

If the Son makes you free, you will be free indeed. (John 8:36)

What does it mean that we are free in Christ? We may find it hard to put into precise words, but instinctively we might sense that it has something to do with an interior release and a limitless potential for life with God. We might sense that this kind of freedom has to do with profound joy and peace or an eager expectation of everything that God has in store.

Freedom is something that God always intended for us. In fact, he gave us the faculties of intellect, emotion, and will so that we could freely decide how we would live. God's intention was that we would use our freedom to turn to him and receive his life within us. However, instead of turning toward him, we used our freedom to turn away from him. The sad result is that we are now no longer free men and women. Instead, we are now enslaved to the power of sin.

As we might expect, there is a cost involved in winning back our freedom. But the good news is that Jesus paid the price necessary to set us free. There is no cost on our part at all! Our freedom from sin is a free gift from God. We only have to ask him for it. Hardly anyone misses an opportunity for a giveaway at the grocery store, but how many days do we go without asking God for freedom from those things that plague us—worry, burdens, fear, or guilt? How foolish it is to continue in bondage when freedom is within our grasp at any moment in the day!

Our God is loving, kind, and faithful. He wants only the best for us and longs for us to come to him every day with open hearts. He delights in revealing himself to us, healing our lives, and restoring us to freedom as his children. In the midst of all the challenges and trials of daily life, let us not lose sight of the One who can free us. Let us come to him confident in his desire to free his children.

"Lord Jesus, I believe that you paid for my freedom from sin and all its effects. I want to accept this freedom that guarantees me limitless access to you and your kingdom. Jesus, set me free!"

John 8:43-50

[43] Why do you not understand what I say? It is because you cannot bear to hear my word. [44] You are of your father the devil, and your will is to do your father's desires. He was a murderer from the beginning, and has nothing to do with the truth, because there is no truth in him. When he lies, he speaks according to his own nature, for he is a liar and the father of lies. [45] But, because I tell the truth, you do not believe me. [46] Which of you convicts me of sin? If I tell the truth, why do you not believe me? [47] He who is of God hears the words of God; the reason why you do not hear them is that you are not of God."
[48] The Jews answered him, "Are we not right in saying that you are a Samaritan and have a demon?" [49] Jesus answered, "I have not a demon; but I honor my Father, and you dishonor me. [50] Yet I do not seek my own glory; there is One who seeks it and he will be the judge."

By referring to the devil as the "father of lies" (John 8:44), Jesus revealed something of crucial importance about Satan: He has no concern for the truth. To achieve his ends, he is willing to use falsehoods, deceptions, even shades of truth. It makes no difference to him, so long as he achieves his goal of destroying the creatures whom God loves.

The devil is an expert in the use of half-truths. For instance, he will try to obscure God's revelation of mercy in the cross of Christ by steering us to see it simply as a measure of our sinfulness. When we look at what Christ suffered for us on the cross, the devil would like us to feel only guilt and condemnation for having added our sins to the load Jesus bore. Then, cheated of the experience of God's forgiveness and love, we walk away without any taste of the new life that God has given us through Jesus' death and resurrection.

On the other hand, Satan is just as willing to obscure the other side of the cross of Christ. He may try to deceive us into looking upon the cross only as an expression of God's mercy so that we would ignore the judgment against sin that the cross expresses. If the devil can get us to forget about God's justice, then he can lure us into sin by whispering, "Go ahead. It's okay: Jesus will always forgive you."

But there is good news—Jesus has overcome the devil (John 12:31). Throughout his life, Jesus kept his eyes fixed on God and listened to his voice continually. That was why, when the devil came to tempt him in the desert, Jesus easily discerned his misquotation of the scriptures and rebuked him (Luke 4:1-13). As we learn to go through each day with Jesus, we too will become able to identify the deceptive voice of the devil. As we keep our hearts and minds fixed on the presence of God, we will be able to see Satan's lies for what they are, and we will learn how to counter them with the truth of the gospel. Every day, let us ask God to fill our minds and hearts with his truth—which is his Son.

"Jesus, I want to know the truth. Teach me how to reject the devil's lies and empty promises. Help me keep my attention on you. Fight for me, Lord, against every attack of the enemy."

John 8:51-59

[51] Truly, truly, I say to you, if any one keeps my word, he will never see death." [52] The Jews said to him, "Now we know that you have a demon. Abraham died, as did the prophets; and you say, 'If any one keeps my word, he will never taste death.' [53] Are you greater than our father Abraham, who died? And the prophets died! Who do you claim to be?" [54] Jesus answered, "If I glorify myself, my glory is nothing; it is my Father who glorifies me, of whom you say that he is your God. [55] But you have not known him; I know him. If I said, I do not know him, I should be a liar like you; but I do know him and I keep his word. [56] Your father Abraham rejoiced that he was to see my day; he saw it and was glad." [57] The Jews then said to him, "You are not yet fifty years old, and have you seen Abraham?" [58] Jesus said to them, "Truly, truly, I say to you, before Abraham was, I am." [59] So they took up stones to throw at him; but Jesus hid himself, and went out of the temple.

Who was this Jesus of Nazareth who claimed that those who kept his word would never see death (John 8:51)? The tension between Jesus and the Jews who opposed him heightened as they tried to come to grips with his identity and his authority to make such a claim. He gave perspective to both issues by saying, "Truly, truly, I say to you, before Abraham was, I am" (8:58). What is the meaning of this enigmatic phrase, and what did Jesus hope to reveal by it?

The phrase, "I am," is the culmination of many "I am" statements that appear throughout scripture concerning Jesus and his divinity.

In John's Gospel, several "I am" phrases appear and form part of a mosaic establishing Jesus' identity and authority: "I am . . . the living bread . . . the light of the world . . . the gate . . . the good shepherd . . . the resurrection and the life . . . the true vine . . . one with the Father."

The Jews with whom Jesus contended did not take scripture lightly. Indeed, they scrupulously attempted to keep every jot and tittle of the law so as to be pleasing to God as they awaited the Messiah. Why then did they not recognize who Jesus was? The problem was that they saw with human eyes and reasoned with human intellects, and this precluded their ability to believe. They were not open to understand Jesus' connection to the Father when he claimed the divine name (Exodus 3:14) for himself by declaring "I am." In fact, they were scandalized by his words (John 10:30-33).

Each of us must consider Jesus' revelation of who he is. A deeper understanding of the truth of Jesus will come as we pray about how he revealed himself. A good place to start would be to consider the "I am" statements listed above. Ask the Holy Spirit to help you understand more fully what these statements reveal about Jesus. Take some extra time today to meditate on some of them. Your prayer will surely reveal more of the rich mosaic before us.

"Holy Spirit, help me to understand more deeply Jesus' revelation of himself when he called himself 'I am.' Many in the world do not believe in him. I pray that my faith, my words, and my life will witness to his glory."

Light of the World

JOHN
9:1-41

John 9:1-12

[1] As he passed by, he saw a man blind from his birth. [2] And his disciples asked him, "Rabbi, who sinned, this man or his parents, that he was born blind?" [3] Jesus answered, "It was not that this man sinned, or his parents, but that the works of God might be made manifest in him. [4] We must work the works of him who sent me, while it is day; night comes, when no one can work. [5] As long as I am in the world, I am the light of the world." [6] As he said this, he spat on the ground and made clay of the spittle and anointed the man's eyes with the clay, [7] saying to him, "Go, wash in the pool of Siloam" (which means Sent). So he went and washed and came back seeing. [8] The neighbors and those who had seen him before as a beggar, said, "Is not this the man who used to sit and beg?" [9] Some said, "It is he"; others said, "No, but he is like him." He said, "I am the man." [10] They said to him, "Then how were your eyes opened?" [11] He answered, "The man called Jesus made clay and anointed my eyes and said to me, 'Go to Siloam and wash'; so I went and washed and received my sight." [12] They said to him, "Where is he?" He said, "I do not know." ▨▨▨

When Adam and Eve sinned and forsook the protection of God, they chose the way that leads to darkness. No longer could they receive the light of God's revelation in their lives. No longer could their hearts be warmed by his presence or their minds be filled with his truth. They and all their children were left without God and would have remained so forever if God had not had mercy and promised salvation.

Those of us who can see may find it even more difficult to grasp the reality of our desperate situation than those who are literally blind. At least they have a physical condition that makes them constantly aware of their true state. We who see the light of day can be tempted to presume that we can see the light of Christ just as easily.

St. Paul thought otherwise. Without Christ, he said, our minds are darkened (Romans 1:21) and hostile to God (8:7). Those who did not know the promises of God were in such a state—living far from God and without hope (Ephesians 2:12). In his gospel, Matthew likened the first announcing of the truth by Christ to a light dawning on those bound in darkness. "The people who sat in darkness have seen a great light, and for those who sat in the region and shadow of death light has dawned" (Matthew 4:16).

Again, St. Peter wrote: "You are a chosen race . . . that you may declare the wonderful deeds of him who called you out of darkness into his marvelous light" (1 Peter 2:9). The Son of God, the Light of the World, came to rescue us from our blindness. Like the blind man in this story, we need the light of Jesus to come into our lives. It was only after Jesus performed this work of healing that the man born blind came to understand the true nature of what had taken place. As this man stood firmly on the truth of his experience, divine understanding—light from heaven—was given to him.

If we want to recognize God's action in our lives, we must pray. No matter who we are, we need forgiveness of our sins; we need freedom from fear; we need to stand joyfully in God's light, under his gaze, and believe that we are his children. Let us kneel before the cross and pray: "I adore you, Jesus, because by your holy cross you have redeemed the world. Let me receive my sight." The Lord will hear our prayer and our eyes will be opened. Such is the promise of our loving Father.

John 9:13-38

[13]   They brought to the Pharisees the man who had formerly been blind. [14] Now it was a sabbath day when Jesus made the clay and opened his eyes. [15] The Pharisees again asked him how he had received his sight. And he said to them, "He put clay on my eyes, and I washed, and I see." [16] Some of the Pharisees said, "This man is not from God, for he does not keep the sabbath." But others said, "How can a man who is a sinner do such signs?" There was a division among them. [17] So they again said to the blind man, "What do you say about him, since he has opened your eyes?" He said, "He is a prophet."

[18]   The Jews did not believe that he had been blind and had received his sight, until they called the parents of the man who had received his sight, [19] and asked them, "Is this your son, who you say was born blind? How then does he now see?" [20] His parents answered, "We know that this is our son, and that he was born blind; [21] but how he now sees we do not know, nor do we know who opened his eyes. Ask him; he is of age, he will speak for himself." [22] His parents said this because they feared the Jews, for the Jews had already agreed that if any one should confess him to be Christ, he was to be put out of the synagogue. [23] Therefore his parents said, "He is of age, ask him."

[24]   So for the second time they called the man who had been blind, and said to him, "Give God the praise; we know that this man is a sinner." [25] He answered, "Whether he is a sinner, I do not know; one thing I know, that though I was blind, now I see." [26] They said to him, "What did he do to you? How did he open your eyes?" [27] He answered them, "I have told you already, and you would not listen. Why do you want to hear it again? Do you too want to become his disciples?" [28] And they reviled him, saying, "You are his disciple, but we are disciples of Moses. [29] We know

that God has spoken to Moses, but as for this man, we do not know where he comes from." [30] The man answered, "Why, this is a marvel! You do not know where he comes from, and yet he opened my eyes. [31] We know that God does not listen to sinners, but if any one is a worshipper of God and does his will, God listens to him. [32] Never since the world began has it been heard that any one opened the eyes of a man born blind. [33] If this man were not from God, he could do nothing." [34] They answered him, "You were born in utter sin, and would you teach us?" And they cast him out. [35] Jesus heard that they had cast him out, and having found him he said, "Do you believe in the Son of man?" [36] He answered, "And who is he, sir, that I may believe in him?" [37] Jesus said to him, "You have seen him, and it is he who speaks to you." [38] He said, "Lord, I believe"; and he worshipped him.

At baptism, Jesus comes to live in our hearts, and we begin to share in the life of God. Heaven is opened to us, and we are made capable of understanding divine realities. Like the blind man healed by Jesus, we cross from darkness to light. But just as that man progressed from knowing his healer simply as "the man called Jesus" to crying out, "Lord, I believe" (John 9:11,38), we too need to grow in Christ. Every day, God gives us opportunities to hold on to Jesus in faith and deepen our belief that he really is God incarnate, capable of destroying all sin and darkness within us.

As we deal with the challenges of life in this world by remaining close to Jesus, we give him the chance to show himself worthy of our trust. Our eyes are opened more fully to his power and his compassion. Our hearts are softened to trust that his commandments are meant for our protection and growth. Our memories are filled with increasing evidence of his faithfulness and provision. Thus, bearing trials patiently and faithfully responding to God's grace is a natural and necessary part of coming to maturity in Christ.

Catherine Marshall, in her book *Meeting God at Every Turn*, wrote:

> Christians do not arrive at any goodness or maturity all at once; our life is always a walk. Even on the straight stretches, for me there had often been such heavy fog that I had to go forward believing that Jesus was with me leading the way. . . . I saw that whenever I had come to Jesus stripped of pretensions with a needy spirit, ready to listen to him and to receive what he had for me, he had met me at my point of need. . . . With him, a seemingly dark and desolate future becomes a joyous new life.

Let us decide today to make the most of every opportunity we are given to grow in the knowledge of God. Let us respond quickly to the prompting of the Holy Spirit, so that the joy and peace of Jesus grow deeper in us today.

"Lord Jesus, I want to know you more deeply. Help me to recognize your work in me day after day. Through all the circumstances of my life, reveal yourself to me. Strengthen my trust in you."

John 9:39-41

[39] Jesus said, "For judgment I came into this world, that those who do not see may see, and that those who see may become blind." [40] Some of the Pharisees near him heard this, and they said to him, "Are we also blind?" [41] Jesus said to them, "If you were blind, you would have no guilt; but now that you say, 'We see,' your guilt remains." ❈❈❈

While Jesus was the one who actually healed the man born blind, John shifts his readers' attention away from Jesus by limiting his appearance to the very beginning and end of the story. He chooses instead to focus on the other characters and their response to Jesus. This strategy propels us to look at this seemingly simple miracle more deeply and reflect on who Jesus really is.

Jesus healed the blind man's vision by sending him to the pool of Siloam. At the same time, he also set the man on a spiritual journey—one that progressed farther every time he was asked to testify about what happened to him. Initially, the blind man simply said he was healed by "the man called Jesus" (John 9:11). Later, he displayed increased insight as he called Jesus "a prophet" (9:17), and still later, one sent "from God" (9:33). Finally, and most profoundly, he proclaimed his full faith in Jesus when he confessed, "Lord, I believe," and worshiped him (9:38). Taking us step by step on the man's journey to faith, John allows us to taste the great gift that Jesus had given him—not just his eyesight, but eternal salvation.

Ironically, the Pharisees grew only more confused and less comprehending even as the blind beggar became more clear and strong in his convictions. They failed to accept the truth they had physically witnessed, precisely because they did not have faith. Consequently, they brought down on themselves their own indict-ment: "If you were blind, you would have no guilt; but now that you say, 'We see,' your guilt remains" (John 9:41).

To some degree, we recognize that the blind man and the Pharisees represent ourselves—caught in darkness, striving toward light. And yet we often resemble the man's parents, too. They dis-tanced themselves from this wonderful healing by resisting all involvement. We, too, can prefer to remain safely in the "gray areas" of indecision.

Let us ask the Holy Spirit to remove the veil from our eyes so that we could see the ways we resist being drawn into the full light of truth. Jesus spread the mud over the blind man's eyes, but the man himself had to respond by washing in the pool. In the same way, we too must respond in faith, bringing ourselves to the living water who is Christ.

The Good Shepherd

JOHN
10:1-42

John 10:1-10

[1] "Truly, truly, I say to you, he who does not enter the sheepfold by the door but climbs in by another way, that man is a thief and a robber; [2] but he who enters by the door is the shepherd of the sheep. [3] To him the gatekeeper opens; the sheep hear his voice, and he calls his own sheep by name and leads them out. [4] When he has brought out all his own, he goes before them, and the sheep follow him, for they know his voice. [5] A stranger they will not follow, but they will flee from him, for they do not know the voice of strangers." [6] This figure Jesus used with them, but they did not understand what he was saying to them.

[7] So Jesus again said to them, "Truly, truly, I say to you, I am the door of the sheep. [8] All who came before me are thieves and robbers; but the sheep did not heed them. [9] I am the door; if any one enters by me, he will be saved, and will go in and out and find pasture. [10] The thief comes only to steal and kill and destroy; I came that they may have life, and have it abundantly."

Jesus' desire for us is that we should have life, and have it to the full (John 10:10). As Christians, we face the question of how we can appropriate this life of God in our own lives. Through Jesus' parable of the sheepfold (10:1-6) and its interpretation (10:7-18), John gives us clear guidance on how we can experience this life.

We can easily sense the loving care which the shepherd has for his sheep and how familiar he is with them. When the shepherd goes to gather his sheep—presumably after they have been penned up for the night—he "calls his own sheep by name and leads them out" (10:3). The custom in Palestine was and still is to give each sheep a name, such as "Long Ear" or "White Nose." When the shepherd "has brought out all his own"—which in itself is not easy because of the crowded condition of the corral—he then "goes before them" to lead them to the pasture (10:4).

For their part, the sheep follow the shepherd because they have heard his voice and are intimately familiar with it (John 10:4). They will not follow a stranger, but will "run from him" because they do not recognize his voice (10:5). While the sheep follow their shepherd willingly, they will not follow anyone else. Indeed, they flee from strangers.

In this parable, Jesus said that he is both the gate and the shepherd (John 10:7,11). While the "thief" comes "to steal and kill and destroy," Jesus asserted that he has come "that they may have life, and have it abundantly" (10:10). If we desire the life Jesus came to give, we need to respond to him as the sheep in the parable respond to the shepherd. We need to follow him and run from any "stranger" who would snatch us from him. Just as the sheep gave a positive, eager response to the shepherd's voice, so too should we follow Jesus and turn away from all that would lead us astray.

When we know the love of our Shepherd for us, such a response is not difficult. Like the shepherd in the parable, Jesus has a loving familiarity with us. He calls us by name and leads us to good pasture. When we know him as our Good Shepherd, we will gladly follow him. And when we do, we will have life, and have it abundantly.

John 10:11-21

[11] I am the good shepherd. The good shepherd lays down his life for the sheep. [12] He who is a hireling and not a shepherd, whose own the sheep are not, sees the wolf coming and leaves the sheep and flees; and the wolf snatches them and scatters them. [13] He flees because he is a hireling and cares nothing for the sheep. [14] I am the good shepherd; I know my own and my own know me, [15] as the Father knows me and I know the Father; and I lay down my life for the sheep. [16] And I have other sheep, that are not of this fold; I must bring them also, and they will heed my voice. So there will be one flock, one shepherd. [17] For this reason the Father loves me, because I lay down my life, that I may take it again. [18] No one takes it from me, but I lay it down of my own accord. I have power to lay it down, and I have power to take it again; this charge I have received from my Father."

[19] There was again a division among the Jews because of these words. [20] Many of them said, "He has a demon, and he is mad; why listen to him?" [21] Others said, "These are not the sayings of one who has a demon. Can a demon open the eyes of the blind?"

Jesus told the Jews that he, the Good Shepherd, would freely lay down his life for us—his sheep (John 10:11). Later on, he would tell his disciples that there is no greater love than to lay down one's life for one's friends (15:13). Jesus perfectly demonstrated that love when he died on the cross, offering up his life for each one of us.

It is staggering to think that if you were the only person in the world, Jesus would still have freely given his life to save you. It was this realization that gave Peter the boldness to tell the chief priests that there is no other name—no person—under heaven capable of bringing us salvation (Acts 4:12).

We have a great cause for rejoicing! God's wisdom, foolish though it seems to the human mind, triumphs even in the darkest moments. Who but God could destine that Jesus, the beloved Son, would be rejected by his own people and abandoned by his closest followers? He was even forsaken by God himself! But this is the unfathomable wisdom of God. He loved us so much that he willingly sacrificed his only Son, whom he loves above anyone or anything else, just to bring us back to his embrace. It is just as the first letter of John declares: "See what love the Father has given us, that we should be called children of God" (1 John 3:1).

During those times when things seem dark and hopeless, we must look to God's loving provision. Even in the unexpected tragedies of life, he is at work, inviting us to draw closer to himself. There are times when his wisdom is so far beyond us that our only response can be faith and trust. In these moments, he asks us to pray: "Jesus, I trust in you." When troubles and darkness surround us, we can proclaim: "Father, you hold me in your hands." When life seems unbearable, we can look to the cross and say: "Lord, you died for me. Help my unbelief."

"Holy Spirit, be my comfort. Be my strength and reveal to me the glorious gospel of Christ. I abandon myself to you and trust you with all that I am and all that I have."

John 10:22-30

22   It was the feast of the Dedication at Jerusalem; 23 it was winter, and Jesus was walking in the temple, in the portico of Solomon. 24 So the Jews gathered round him and said to him, "How long will you keep us in suspense? If you are the Christ, tell us plainly." 25 Jesus answered them, "I told you, and you do not believe. The works that I do in my Father's name, they bear witness to me; 26 but you do not believe, because you do not belong to my sheep. 27 My sheep hear my voice, and I know them, and they follow me; 28 and I give them eternal life, and they shall never perish, and no one shall snatch them out of my hand. 29 My Father, who has given them to me, is greater than all, and no one is able to snatch them out of the Father's hand. 30 I and the Father are one."

I and the Father are one. (John 10:30)

What could be a more profound statement? You can just imagine how Jesus' hearers might have responded to this truth. Some wanted to stone him for claiming equality with God (John 10:31; see 5:18). Others were probably so astounded that they began to reevaluate everything Jesus had said and done in light of such a claim.

None of Jesus' listeners could ever imagine coming face to face with God himself. Yet Jesus was holding out the promise of a relationship that would impact their lives forever. He told his disciples later on, "He who has seen me has seen the Father" (14:9). In everything he said or did, Jesus revealed another dimension of God their heavenly Father. And with each revelation, the loving, just, and compassionate character of the Father became clearer and clearer.

Whenever he healed, Jesus revealed his Father's compassion (John 9:1-7). He revealed his Father's mercy when he forgave the woman caught in adultery (8:1-11) and offered living water to the woman from Samaria (4:1-42). He demonstrated the awesome power of God when he calmed the storm that threatened and terrified the disciples (6:15-21). He defied the laws of nature, walking on turbulent waters and passing through solid walls (20:19). He showed God's righteousness when he overturned the merchants' tables in the temple (2:13-21). Time and time again, he revealed the wisdom of God as he deftly answered the religious leaders' attempts to trap him in his own words (8:25-30; 10:32-38).

With such promising truths before us, we can take great comfort. Through Jesus, not only can we know the Father personally, we can belong solely to him—now and forever. Let us listen to Jesus' promise: "My Father . . . is greater than all, and no one is able to snatch them out of the Father's hand" (John 10:29).

"Father, we open our hearts to you. Teach us what it means to be your children, protected and cared for by your Son, the Good Shepherd. Help us to turn to Jesus continually because he is our protector."

John 10:31-42

[31] The Jews took up stones again to stone him. [32] Jesus answered them, "I have shown you many good works from the Father; for which of these do you stone me?" [33] The Jews answered him, "It is not for a good work that we stone you but for blasphemy; because you, being a man, make yourself God." [34] Jesus answered them, "Is it

not written in your law, 'I said, you are gods'? [35] If he called them gods to whom the word of God came (and scripture cannot be broken), [36] do you say of him whom the Father consecrated and sent into the world, 'You are blaspheming,' because I said, 'I am the Son of God'? [37] If I am not doing the works of my Father, then do not believe me; [38] but if I do them, even though you do not believe me, believe the works, that you may know and understand that the Father is in me and I am in the Father." [39] Again they tried to arrest him, but he escaped from their hands.

[40] He went away again across the Jordan to the place where John at first baptized, and there he remained. [41] And many came to him; and they said, "John did no sign, but everything that John said about this man was true." [42] And many believed in him there.

How could Jesus' own people oppose him so strongly? Shouldn't it have been easy for them to accept him? But his was a very hard teaching, especially for those Jews who took pride in their position as God's chosen people. We have only to think of the apostle Paul who, prior to his conversion, simply could not accept that the gospel preached by Peter and the apostles—themselves Jews— was the true fulfillment of all Israel's hopes.

It may baffle us that so many of Jesus' fellow Jews rejected him, yet we should always remember that opposition to Jesus resides within every human heart, including our own. The Jews had seen so many of Jesus' miracles and heard his teachings and parables, but when they were confronted with their own sin and need for repentance, it became hard to accept him. No matter how many miracles we may see, they will never be enough to convince us. Something has to change within our hearts.

This message strikes a chord in all of us. God wants us to recognize our opposition to him so that through repentance we can turn to him and know freedom. God wants us to examine our consciences and see the opposition we carry in our hearts. We can ask the Holy Spirit to probe us and help us see the hardness within us. It may manifest itself in anger or bitterness. Perhaps envy or a critical tongue give us away. It may be more subtle, such as thinking we are better than others or taking pride in our religious observances. Whatever our sins, they all point to one central reality: opposition to Jesus and his gospel.

That is why the church offers the Sacrament of Reconciliation. God wants to show us our sins, not to condemn us, but to give us new life and freedom. The freedom we can experience when we confess our sins enables us to walk more closely with the Lord. Let us not miss out on any opportunity for a closer walk with the Lord.

"Holy Spirit, probe my heart today. Show me ways that I seek to justify myself and fail to acknowledge my sin. I confess that I am a sinner. I accept Jesus as my only salvation. Empower me to walk with him and experience his freeing love."

Resurrection and Life

JOHN
11:1-57

John 11:1-27

¹ Now a certain man was ill, Lazarus of Bethany, the village of Mary and her sister Martha. ² It was Mary who anointed the Lord with ointment and wiped his feet with her hair, whose brother Lazarus was ill. ³ So the sisters sent to him, saying, "Lord, he whom you love is ill." ⁴ But when Jesus heard it he said, "This illness is not unto death; it is for the glory of God, so that the Son of God may be glorified by means of it."

⁵ Now Jesus loved Martha and her sister and Lazarus. ⁶ So when he heard that he was ill, he stayed two days longer in the place where he was. ⁷ Then after this he said to the disciples, "Let us go into Judea again." ⁸ The disciples said to him, "Rabbi, the Jews were but now seeking to stone you, and are you going there again?" ⁹ Jesus answered, "Are there not twelve hours in the day? If any one walks in the day, he does not stumble, because he sees the light of this world. ¹⁰ But if any one walks in the night, he stumbles, because the light is not in him." ¹¹ Thus he spoke, and then he said to them, "Our friend Lazarus has fallen asleep, but I go to awake him out of sleep." ¹² The disciples said to him, "Lord, if he has fallen asleep, he will recover." ¹³ Now Jesus had spoken of his death, but they thought that he meant taking rest in sleep. ¹⁴ Then Jesus told them plainly, "Lazarus is dead; ¹⁵ and for your sake I am glad that I was not there, so that you may believe. But let us go to him." ¹⁶ Thomas, called the Twin, said to his fellow disciples, "Let us also go, that we may die with him."

¹⁷ Now when Jesus came, he found that Lazarus had already been in the tomb four days. ¹⁸ Bethany was near Jerusalem, about two miles off, ¹⁹ and many of the Jews had come to Martha and Mary to console them concerning their brother. ²⁰ When Martha heard that Jesus was coming, she went and met him, while Mary sat in the house. ²¹ Martha said to Jesus, "Lord, if you had been here, my brother would not have died. ²² And even now I know that whatever

you ask from God, God will give you." ^{23} Jesus said to her, "Your brother will rise again." ^{24} Martha said to him, "I know that he will rise again in the resurrection at the last day." ^{25} Jesus said to her, "I am the resurrection and the life; he who believes in me, though he die, yet shall he live, ^{26} and whoever lives and believes in me shall never die. Do you believe this?" ^{27} She said to him, "Yes, Lord; I believe that you are the Christ, the Son of God, he who is coming into the world."

God's word proclaims the twofold promise of life available to all who respond to Jesus Christ. It is a life that can be lived right now and a life that will never end. In the earliest Old Testament writings, there was no expression of a belief in life after death. But around time of the exile, through the prophet Ezekiel (37:1-14) and in the Book of Job (19:25), we glimpse a vague shadow of the idea of a God who could raise the dead.

By the second century B.C., this concept had blossomed into a belief among some Jews that God would grant eternal life to the righteous (Daniel 12:2-3; 2 Maccabees 7:9). Jesus himself promised Martha: "Your brother will rise again" (John 11:23). Martha, in turn, professed her faith in the resurrection of Lazarus on the last day. But Jesus led Martha beyond an acceptance in the hope of life after death to the reality of himself as the source of Lazarus' new life (11:24-26).

John paints Lazarus as a symbol of all of us—dead to God and bound by sin. Like Lazarus, each of us is loved by Jesus. He weeps over our suffering and calls us by name to come out of our tombs of unbelief, self-centeredness, and futility. To those who saw or heard of it, the raising of Lazarus was a sign of Jesus' power over death. But Jesus also knew that Lazarus would die again at some point in the future.

The new thing would come about through the cross of Christ. Jesus' resurrection is not meant only to resuscitate us. Jesus' resurrection ensures our passage to a transformed life—beginning the moment we place our trust in him as Lord and Savior.

Paul described how this new life is possible: When we die with Christ in baptism, we also rise with him (Romans 6:8). The same power of the Holy Spirit that raised Jesus from the dead is at work within all believers (8:11). We are changed from a natural existence so that we can live spiritually. It is not a life we possess in and of ourselves, but a life that has its source in God. He promises that as we put our faith in the Holy Spirit, we will be empowered to live this life in a way that is pleasing to him.

Jesus' words to Martha that her brother would rise are the same words he speaks to us every day. Yes, we will rise with Jesus on the last day, but even now we can rise with him daily as we die with him. He has promised it and we can experience it as we unite ourselves to him.

John 11:28-44

28 When she had said this, she went and called her sister Mary, saying quietly, "The Teacher is here and is calling for you." 29 And when she heard it, she rose quickly and went to him. 30 Now Jesus had not yet come to the village, but was still in the place where Martha had met him. 31 When the Jews who were with her in the house, consoling her, saw Mary rise quickly and go out, they followed her, supposing that she was going to the tomb to weep there. 32 Then Mary, when she came where Jesus was and saw him, fell at his feet, saying to him, "Lord, if you had been here, my brother would not have died." 33 When Jesus saw her weeping, and

the Jews who came with her also weeping, he was deeply moved in spirit and troubled; [34] and he said, "Where have you laid him?" They said to him, "Lord, come and see." [35] Jesus wept. [36] So the Jews said, "See how he loved him!" [37] But some of them said, "Could not he who opened the eyes of the blind man have kept this man from dying?"

[38] Then Jesus, deeply moved again, came to the tomb; it was a cave, and a stone lay upon it. [39] Jesus said, "Take away the stone." Martha, the sister of the dead man, said to him, "Lord, by this time there will be an odor, for he has been dead four days." [40] Jesus said to her, "Did I not tell you that if you would believe you would see the glory of God?" [41] So they took away the stone. And Jesus lifted up his eyes and said, "Father, I thank you that you have heard me. [42] I knew that you hear me always, but I have said this on account of the people standing by, that they may believe that you did send me." [43] When he had said this, he cried with a loud voice, "Lazarus, come out." [44] The dead man came out, his hands and feet bound with bandages, and his face wrapped with a cloth. Jesus said to them, "Unbind him, and let him go."

When Jesus told Martha that Lazarus would rise, she replied, "I know that he will rise again in the resurrection at the last day" (John 11:24). In spite of Martha's doubts, Jesus proceeded to raise Lazarus immediately. Like Martha, we sometimes push God's power so far into the future that we cannot acknowledge his power at work in us here and now. He gives us life now through baptism and a life of faith just as clearly as he raised Lazarus from the tomb.

In baptism we rise with Jesus to begin a journey where we too will die, but where we will also rise body and soul to eternal life at the last judgment. Lazarus was such a powerful witness to Jesus' life-giving power that the Jewish leaders wanted to kill him (John 12:10). Commenting on this, St. Augustine wryly wrote that if they had killed Lazarus, Jesus would have simply raised him again (*Homilies on John*, 50.14)!

Almost six hundred years before the birth of Christ, the prophet Ezekiel had a powerful vision of God's Spirit raising his people to new life. In the valley of dry bones, he prophesied, "O spirit, breathe into these slain that they may come to life" (Ezekiel 37:9, NAB). Like Lazarus' resurrection, Ezekiel's vision foretells the new life God gives us today as well as our final resurrection from the dead. For our part, we must accept the grace of baptism if we want God's grace to take root in our lives.

An ancient Jewish rabbi, Judah ben Simon, commented on Ezekiel's vision of dry bones to teach that it is our responsibility to listen to God's voice: "[God] said to them, 'At first I told you, Hear ye the word of the Lord, O house of Jacob (Jeremiah 2:4), and you did not listen; but now you have listened. When you were alive you did not listen, but now that you are dead you have listened!' " (*Ecclesiastes Rabba*, IV.3.1). In other words, he taught that we should listen and accept God's call in this life because we will have no choice except to listen to God's voice of judgment at the last day. Let us pray that at the final resurrection we will be in God's favor.

John 11:45-57

[45] Many of the Jews therefore, who had come with Mary and had seen what he did, believed in him; [46] but some of them went to the Pharisees and told them what Jesus had done. [47] So the chief priests and the Pharisees gathered the council, and said, "What are we to do? For this man performs many signs. [48] If we let him go on thus, every one will believe in him, and the Romans will come and destroy both our holy place and our nation." [49] But one of them, Caiaphas, who was high priest that year, said to them, "You know nothing at all; [50] you do not understand that it is expedient for you that one man should die for the people, and that the whole nation should not perish." [51] He did not say this of his own accord, but being high priest that year he prophesied that Jesus should die for the nation, [52] and not for the nation only, but to gather into one the children of God who are scattered abroad. [53] So from that day on they took counsel how to put him to death.

[54] Jesus therefore no longer went about openly among the Jews, but went from there to the country near the wilderness, to a town called Ephraim; and there he stayed with the disciples.

[55] Now the Passover of the Jews was at hand, and many went up from the country to Jerusalem before the Passover, to purify themselves. [56] They were looking for Jesus and saying to one another as they stood in the temple, "What do you think? That he will not come to the feast?" [57] Now the chief priests and the Pharisees had given orders that if any one knew where he was, he should let them know, so that they might arrest him.

As we read about the events leading to Jesus' death, it might appear as though the Jewish leaders and Roman authorities had the upper hand and were in control of the events that were about to unfold. In reality, however, God was behind everything that happened as he firmly guided his plan to completion. He even used Caiaphas, Israel's high priest that year, to prophesy that Jesus would die for the nation. Caiaphas meant to say nothing more than that killing Jesus was the politically expedient thing to do—but God had other plans.

As Jesus approached his final week, he remained focused on the Father's plan, even as the conspiracy against him grew. John tells us that many of the Jews who had witnessed Jesus raise Lazarus from the dead came to believe in him, but that others reported him to the Pharisees (John 11:45-46). Nevertheless, despite the darkening of his situation, Jesus continued to rely on the Spirit to keep him close to his Father and enable him to obey.

God still sends signs to his church to help his children grow in their faith. And, as in Jesus' day, some will open their hearts and believe that Jesus is the Messiah, while others will question and doubt out of fear. Still, whatever the age or circumstance, God will continue to advance his kingdom through those who trust in him despite the difficulties.

Let us ask the Holy Spirit to open our hearts. Let us hold fast to the path God has set before us. Each path is unique; each has its own shades of darkness and challenge. Still, they all lead to Jesus, our one hope and comfort. Every time we ponder the mysteries of our redemption, we can grow in love for Jesus and in our desire to remain obedient to his calling. God has called all of us to advance his kingdom. Let us ask the Spirit to reveal to us our potential in him.

"Father, thank you for sending Jesus to be the sign of your love for us. Open our eyes that we might see the continued presence of the Holy Spirit in the world today."

The Turning Point

JOHN
12:1-50

John 12:1-11

[1] Six days before the Passover, Jesus came to Bethany, where Lazarus was, whom Jesus had raised from the dead. [2] There they made him a supper; Martha served, and Lazarus was one of those at table with him. [3] Mary took a pound of costly ointment of pure nard and anointed the feet of Jesus and wiped his feet with her hair; and the house was filled with the fragrance of the ointment. [4] But Judas Iscariot, one of his disciples (he who was to betray him), said, [5] "Why was this ointment not sold for three hundred denarii and given to the poor?" [6] This he said, not that he cared for the poor but because he was a thief, and as he had the money box he used to take what was put into it. [7] Jesus said, "Let her alone, let her keep it for the day of my burial. [8] The poor you always have with you, but you do not always have me."

[9] When the great crowd of the Jews learned that he was there, they came, not only on account of Jesus but also to see Lazarus, whom he had raised from the dead. [10] So the chief priests planned to put Lazarus also to death, [11] because on account of him many of the Jews were going away and believing in Jesus.

The account of Mary anointing Jesus at Bethany before his Passion is so important that it appears in three gospels (Matthew 26:6-13; Mark 14:3-9; John 12:1-11). As Jesus' hour approached, he was prepared for his burial by the "good service" that Mary provided by anointing his feet with precious and expensive oil.

The story depicts two very different ways of responding to Jesus. On the one hand is Mary, who surrendered something of great material value in order to honor Jesus. A denarius is valued at one day's wages, which means that the perfume Mary poured onto Jesus' feet was worth nearly a year's wages! On the other hand is Judas, the betrayer of the Lord, who questioned Mary's action and sought to sell the perfume and keep the money for himself.

Judas' question about why the perfume was wasted to anoint Jesus' feet (John 12:5) gives us pause for reflection. We may be inclined to think, along with Judas, that it is a waste to spend our lives on Jesus. We could reasonably give to him from our surplus of time or material goods. Many of us would readily offer to God that which is easy to give and not go any further. But Mary's act of "wasting" her greatest treasure on Jesus confronts such thinking. It demonstrates that complete surrender to Christ brings great honor to him, joy to the giver, and encouragement to the entire church. John tells us that "the house was filled with the fragrance of the ointment" (12:3). Mary's surrender not only affected herself and Jesus, but the whole house and everyone in it.

As we love and serve Jesus with our lives—both in prayer and in service to the poor, sick, and needy—our actions are like Mary's ointment poured out on the Lord. The love for Jesus that underlies such actions and our choice to lavish our lives on him and his people join us to Mary and all those throughout history who have "wasted" themselves on Jesus. May the sacrifice of our lives fill our homes, our churches, and the whole world with the fragrance of loving surrender to Christ.

"Lord, move in my heart as you moved in Mary's heart. I offer everything I am to you. Help me to see the immense value of spending my life on you, and may my actions bring joy to your heart."

John 12:12-19

[12]   The next day a great crowd who had come to the feast heard that Jesus was coming to Jerusalem. [13] So they took branches of palm trees and went out to meet him, crying, "Hosanna! Blessed is he who comes in the name of the Lord, even the King of Israel!" [14] And Jesus found a young ass and sat upon it; as it is written, [15] "Fear not, daughter of Zion; behold, your king is coming, sitting on an ass's colt!" [16] His disciples did not understand this at first; but when Jesus was glorified, then they remembered that this had been written of him and had been done to him. [17] The crowd that had been with him when he called Lazarus out of the tomb and raised him from the dead bore witness.

[18]   The reason why the crowd went to meet him was that they heard he had done this sign. [19] The Pharisees then said to one another, "You see that you can do nothing; look, the world has gone after him."

For the disciples, the pieces of the puzzle came together after Jesus died and rose. With the help of the Holy Spirit, they looked back over their time with their Master and came to understand the significance of many of the dramatic things he had said and done. Jesus' triumphal entry into Jerusalem, when the crowds hailed him as a king (John 12:13), was one such occasion. Once Jesus was glorified and the Holy Spirit poured out, the disciples could see that, as Jesus rode the donkey into Jerusalem, he fulfilled the prophecy in Zechariah 9:9: "Lo, your king comes to you . . . humble and riding on an ass." Jesus truly was the King of Israel and the Redeemer of his people.

It was Jesus' death, resurrection, and ascension that enabled the Spirit to be poured out and the disciples to come to grasp God's plan.

In the light of the risen Lord, and through revelation by the Holy Spirit, they finally understood what Jesus meant, for instance, when he said that he would raise the temple in three days (John 2:19-22) or when he insisted on washing the apostles' feet (13:5-7).

For us too, everything changes when we encounter the risen Christ. The scriptures come to life, just as they did for the disciples on the road to Emmaus when the risen Jesus interpreted them (Luke 24:32). We begin to think differently about our lives and about this world. We experience a desire to worship God, especially in the celebration of the Eucharist. We sense that God has a plan for us and a role of service in his kingdom on earth, and we want to do our part. Realizing that Jesus surrendered his life so that we could live, we want to offer our lives back to him.

The glorified Christ, seen by the apostles after his resurrection, is as real today in our world as he was two thousand years ago. Let us humbly open our hearts to him and acknowledge our need for him. Let us ask the Holy Spirit to show Jesus to us in his risen glory. Then, like the people along the road into Jerusalem, we will cry, "Hosanna! Blessed is he who comes in the name of the Lord!" (John 12:13).

"Lord Jesus, you died and rose again to give me new life. Praise to you! Let me know you in your glory and power. Open my mind and heart to understand your word, and enable me to live in your presence always."

John 12:20-33

20 Now among those who went up to worship at the feast were some Greeks. 21 So these came to Philip, who was from Beth-saida in Galilee, and said to him, "Sir, we wish to see Jesus." 22 Philip went and told Andrew; Andrew went with Philip and they told

Jesus. [23] And Jesus answered them, "The hour has come for the Son of man to be glorified. [24] Truly, truly, I say to you, unless a grain of wheat falls into the earth and dies, it remains alone; but if it dies, it bears much fruit. [25] He who loves his life loses it, and he who hates his life in this world will keep it for eternal life. [26] If any one serves me, he must follow me; and where I am, there shall my servant be also; if any one serves me, the Father will honor him. [27] "Now is my soul troubled. And what shall I say? 'Father, save me from this hour? No, for this purpose I have come to this hour. [28] Father, glorify your name." Then a voice came from heaven, "I have glorified it, and I will glorify it again." [29] The crowd standing by heard it and said that it had thundered. Others said, "An angel has spoken to him." [30] Jesus answered, "This voice has come for your sake, not for mine. [31] Now is the judgment of this world, now shall the ruler of this world be cast out; [32] and I, when I am lifted up from the earth, will draw all men to myself." [33] He said this to show by what death he was to die. ✹✹✹

Picture for moment a common grain of wheat. It appears inert and lifeless, yet we know that within its hard, outer shell is a germ of life waiting to come forth. We also know that the only way this life can be brought out is by placing the seed in the darkness of the earth. Silently, life springs forth and produces much fruit.

John tied this theme of the seed dying to that of Jesus' "hour"— the moment toward which Jesus' whole life had been directed. This moment was not the result of haphazard events and forces; it was an hour over which Jesus had absolute control. It was his hour, the hour when, like the grain of wheat, he would die and bear much fruit. Jesus was the seed, and his hour was the time of his passion, death, and resurrection. Because he chose obedience to the Father's will, the rich harvest he was to bear was nothing less than the salvation for all people.

It is clear that we cannot understand these words as just an exhortation to deny ourselves. To do so would be to fail to grasp the absolute necessity of Jesus' death. Apart from his sacrificial death, there can be no fruit. The key to our bearing fruit is to recognize that, as believers, we have died with Jesus. The Holy Spirit will reveal this truth to us as we put to death those things that stand in the way of our life in Christ. As we do, we will see new life springing forth from death.

This is why Jesus spoke of us as "following" him (John 12:26)— it's a following that involves an embrace of his life and an imitation of his character. Reflecting on Jesus' call for his disciples to follow him, St. Bernard of Clairvaux (1090-1153) once wrote:

How few there are, Lord, who wish to follow you and yet there is not one who does not wish to reach you. . . . All men therefore wish to enjoy you, but not to the extent of following your example; they will reign with you but not suffer with you (*On the Song of Songs*, Sermon 21.2).

Jesus has chosen us to bear fruit (John 15:16). We need to remember this truth when our hour comes and the Spirit leads us to lay before the cross our selfishness, pride, fear, and resentment. By accepting the Father's will for us, we will know the resurrected life of Jesus. Our hour will be a time of glorification.

John 12:34-50

34 The crowd answered him, "We have heard from the law that the Christ remains for ever. How can you say that the Son of man must be lifted up? Who is this Son of man?" 35 Jesus said to them, "The light is with you for a little longer. Walk while you have the light, lest the darkness overtake you; he who walks in the darkness does not know where he goes. 36 While you have the light, believe in the light, that you may become sons of light."

When Jesus had said this, he departed and hid himself from them. 37 Though he had done so many signs before them, yet they did not believe in him; 38 it was that the word spoken by the prophet Isaiah might be fulfilled: "Lord, who has believed our report, and to whom has the arm of the Lord been revealed?" 39 Therefore they could not believe. For Isaiah again said, 40 "He has blinded their eyes and hardened their heart, lest they should see with their eyes and perceive with their heart, and turn for me to heal them." 41 Isaiah said this because he saw his glory and spoke of him. 42 Nevertheless many even of the authorities believed in him, but for fear of the Pharisees they did not confess it, lest they should be put out of the synagogue: 43 for they loved the praise of men more than the praise of God.

44 And Jesus cried out and said, "He who believes in me, believes not in me but in him who sent me. 45 And he who sees me sees him who sent me. 46 I have come as light into the world, that whoever believes in me may not remain in darkness. 47 If any one hears my sayings and does not keep them, I do not judge him; for I did not come to judge the world but to save the world. 48 He who rejects me and does not receive my sayings has a judge; the word that I have spoken will be his judge on the last day. 49 For I have not spoken on my own authority; the Father who sent me has himself given me commandment what to say and what to speak. 50 And I know that

his commandment is eternal life. What I say, therefore, I say as the Father has bidden me." ✠✠✠

T he first part of John's Gospel (chapters 1-12) is often called the "Book of Signs." These chapters describe Jesus' life among the people as he performed miracles that manifested his glory and witnessed to his divine nature. He changed water into wine at Cana (2:1-11), healed the sick and the blind (5:2-18; 9:1-41), multiplied the loaves and fishes (6:1-14), and raised Lazarus from the dead (11:1-44). Through signs like these, Jesus sought to draw people to believe in him: "When the Christ appears, will he do more signs than this man has done?" (7:31).

In the "Book of Glory" (chapters 13 through 21), Jesus opened his heart to his disciples—washing their feet (13:3-16), promising them the Holy Spirit (14:16-17), and praying for their unity (17:20-26). All Jesus' words in this second part lead us to the greatest of signs, the Son of God lifted up on the cross (3:14; 8:28; 12:32).

Common to both books is the way in which Jesus sought to reveal his Father. "He who believes in me, believes not in me but in him who sent me" (John 12:44). Jesus received his identity, his authority, and his mission from his Father. He was a reflection of the Father's love, and his entire purpose on earth was to do what the Father called him to do (12:50).

Jesus didn't come to just dazzle people or to coerce them to pay him homage; he performed these signs to bring people to faith. Through them, he wanted to reveal the Father's heart. He wants all of us to recognize the light of God, even in the midst of sin and darkness (John 12:46). He became man so that we could see God with a human face. Not ashamed to call us his brothers and sisters, he kneels beside us as we lift our hearts to our Father in prayer. In everything he does, Jesus' intention is that we would experience the Father's love for us—the love that brought him into the world as the Lamb whose death brings us life.

"Jesus, you sent the Holy Spirit to teach us about the love of your Father. Deepen the life of the Spirit in us, so that we may know, love, and serve the Father as you do."

The Last Supper

JOHN
13:1-38

John 13:1-15

[1] Now before the feast of the Passover, when Jesus knew that his hour had come to depart out of this world to the Father, having loved his own who were in the world, he loved them to the end. [2] And during supper, when the devil had already put it into the heart of Judas Iscariot, Simon's son, to betray him, [3] Jesus, knowing that the Father had given all things into his hands, and that he had come from God and was going to God, [4] rose from supper, laid aside his garments, and girded himself with a towel. [5] Then he poured water into a basin, and began to wash the disciples' feet, and to wipe them with the towel with which he was girded. [6] He came to Simon Peter; and Peter said to him, "Lord, do you wash my feet?" [7] Jesus answered him, "What I am doing you do not know now, but afterward you will understand." [8] Peter said to him, "You shall never wash my feet." Jesus answered him, "If I do not wash you, you have no part in me." [9] Simon Peter said to him, "Lord, not my feet only but also my hands and my head!" [10] Jesus said to him, "He who has bathed does not need to wash, except for his feet, but he is clean all over; and you are clean, but not every one of you." [11] For he knew who was to betray him; that was why he said, "You are not all clean."

[12] When he had washed their feet, and taken his garments, and resumed his place, he said to them, "Do you know what I have done to you? [13] You call me Teacher and Lord; and you are right, for so I am. [14] If I then, your Lord and Teacher, have washed your feet, you also ought to wash one another's feet. [15] For I have given you an example, that you also should do as I have done to you."

J esus did not come into our midst demanding honor and homage. Rather, he came in humility, desiring only to reveal the love of God to everyone. Even on the night when he was to be betrayed by one of his own, his greatest concern was that his disciples be assured of his love. He knew that if they were confident of his care for them, they would be more free to love others and share his words with them.

Jesus' heart is the same yesterday, today, and forever. In love, he invites all of us to an intimate meal with him, where we receive his flesh and blood in the Eucharist. As we partake of this divine food, Jesus comes to us to "wash our feet," cleansing away the cares and strains of life in this fallen world. He comes to tell us that we are his beloved. He comes to fill us with his love and to empower us to desire the best for our brothers and sisters in Christ.

It is humbling to allow someone to take care of our basic needs, let alone kneel before us and wash our feet. The very idea clashes with the pride we derive from doing everything ourselves or thinking that we have to earn such love. No doubt Peter experienced this as he exclaimed, "You will never wash my feet!" Imagine his surprise when Jesus responded, "If I do not wash you, you have no part in me" (John 13:8).

Jesus knows how deeply we need his love if we are to experience the joy of living for him. He kneels before us now—today—ready to wash us, love us, and fill us. Can we allow him to do this? By washing our feet through the Eucharist, he restores us to the Father. He strengthens us, softens the hardness of our hearts, and heals us. And it is this very love of God that compels us to walk as Jesus did, sharing his love with others in humility and mercy.

"Heavenly Father, I see the perfection of your love for us in your Son, Jesus, who emptied himself so that I might be filled. I open my heart to receive all that you want to give. Holy Spirit, open my eyes to see Jesus in my midst. Mold me into one who demonstrates your love to everyone you bring into my life."

John 13:16-20

[16] "Truly, truly, I say to you, a servant is not greater than his master; nor is he who is sent greater than he who sent him. [17] If you know these things, blessed are you if you do them. [18] I am not speaking of you all; I know whom I have chosen; it is that the scripture may be fulfilled, 'He who ate my bread has lifted his heel against me.' [19] I tell you this now, before it takes place, that when it does take place you may believe that I am he. [20] Truly, truly, I say to you, he who receives any one whom I send receives me; and he who receives me receives him who sent me."

Jesus began his last meal with his disciples by humbling himself and washing their feet (John 13:1-16). On the following day, he would display his servant's heart in a far more powerful way by laying down his life for all of us.

Such a perfect sacrifice is love in its purest form because it is a reflection of the love that exists within the Trinity. The Father so loves the Son that he forever pours his life and goodness into him. The Son, filled with love for the Father, returns that love through his humility and obedience, even to death on the cross. The Spirit completes the circle by ever glorifying the Father and Son, revealing the goodness of God to all creation. This *agapé* love—love characterized by a continuous outpouring—is the very heart of the communion of the Trinity. And, marvelously, it is a communion in which we are all invited to participate.

We enter into this communion as we allow the Lord to serve us. Jesus told Peter: "If I do not wash you, you have no part in me" (John 13:8). Like Peter, we can be so accustomed to a life of self-sufficiency that we find it hard to let Jesus serve us. It is far better, we think, to serve him. But God wants to lift us out of sin and gather us into his arms. Perhaps we shrink from the thought of Jesus serving us because we sense that we are not worthy. Yet this is the very reason why he came to us: We cannot cleanse ourselves.

Jesus told his disciples, "If you know these things, blessed are you if you do them" (John 13:17). As we accept the Lord's self-giving love and his servant's heart, we are filled with the ability and desire to serve others in the same way. It is a great blessing to be able to imitate Christ, to manifest his love and humility to the world. This is our privilege because, like Jesus, we are beloved sons and daughters of the Father.

"Father, give me the grace to glimpse the love that exists in the Trinity. Help me to receive your Son into my heart each day and allow him to wash me in his mercy. By your Spirit, fill my heart with the same self-giving love, and send me into the world to wash your people's feet."

John 13:21-32

^{21} When Jesus had thus spoken, he was troubled in spirit, and testified, "Truly, truly, I say to you, one of you will betray me." ^{22} The disciples looked at one another, uncertain of whom he spoke. ^{23} One of his disciples, whom Jesus loved, was lying close to the breast of Jesus; ^{24} so Simon Peter beckoned to him and said, "Tell us who it is of whom he speaks." ^{25} So lying thus, close to the breast of Jesus, he said to him, "Lord, who is it?" ^{26} Jesus answered, "It is he to whom I shall give this morsel when I have dipped it." So when he had dipped the morsel, he gave it to Judas, the son of Simon Iscariot. ^{27} Then after the morsel, Satan entered into him.

Jesus said to him, "What you are going to do, do quickly." ^{28} Now
no one at the table knew why he said this to him. ^{29} Some thought
that, because Judas had the money box, Jesus was telling him, "Buy
what we need for the feast"; or, that he should give something to the
poor. ^{30} So, after receiving the morsel, he immediately went out;
and it was night.
^{31} When he had gone out, Jesus said, "Now is the Son of man
glorified, and in him God is glorified; ^{32} if God is glorified in him,
God will also glorify him in himself, and glorify him at once."

> *So, after receiving the morsel, he immediately went out;*
> *and it was night. (John 13:30)*

These words draw us into the terrible moment—Judas' betrayal.
Together with his closest friends, Jesus shared a meal with this
one whom he had also called to follow him. Knowing full well
his betrayer's scheme, Jesus nevertheless told Judas, "What you are
going to do, do quickly" (John 13:27). Jesus thus let the events unfold
that would culminate in his agonizing death at Calvary.

Here is the great irony of Holy Week. In committing himself to
the cross, Jesus declared the hidden truth about his decision: "Now
is the Son of man glorified, and in him God is glorified; if God is glorified in him, God will also glorify him in himself, and glorify him at
once" (John 13:31-32).

Here is the paradox of the divine plan of salvation. The Almighty
Son of God became flesh so that he could die for our sins. In his death
is the vindication of the wisdom of God, the manifestation of God's
merciful love to the whole world. Jesus saw his glory, and the glory
of his Father, in the path of betrayal by a friend, humiliation by his
people, condemnation by his leaders, and execution by a weak gov-

ernment official. Jesus was glorified in being scourged, beaten, spat upon, and mocked, because in this he accepted the will of the Father—that he should taste death on behalf of his wayward brothers and sisters. Because he endured abandonment, desolation, and rejection out of obedience to God, he is now seated at God's right hand, interceding for all humanity.

At history's critical juncture, when all our lives hung in the balance, Jesus' obedience to the Father shone out with beauty and majesty. Jesus considered submission to God—the thing that demons and fallen men revile—as honor and triumph. His obedience overturned all preconceptions and proved God to be just and merciful. His complete love for the Father unveiled God's complete love for the world. It revealed a Father for whom no price was too great to ransom his children.

"O King of kings, you accepted a crown of thorns, a mantle of suffering, and a cloak of death for my sake. O happy exchange, that won so great a salvation! To you, the Mighty One who took flesh, the Immortal One who died for sinners, be all glory and honor!"

John 13:33-38

[33] Little children, yet a little while I am with you. You will seek me; and as I said to the Jews so now I say to you, 'Where I am going you cannot come.' [34] A new commandment I give to you, that you love one another; even as I have loved you, that you also love one another. [35] By this all men will know that you are my disciples, if you have love for one another."

³⁶ Simon Peter said to him, "Lord, where are you going?" Jesus answered, "Where I am going you cannot follow me now; but you shall follow afterward." ³⁷ Peter said to him, "Lord, why cannot I follow you now? I will lay down my life for you." ³⁸ Jesus answered, "Will you lay down your life for me? Truly, truly, I say to you, the cock will not crow, till you have denied me three times.

Everyone will know you are my disciples,
if you have love for one another. (John 13:35)

How simple the gospel is! It proclaims a love that has the power to change the world—the love of God poured into human hearts by the Holy Spirit. This is the love of God that flows between us as we lay down our lives for one another. As we lift our hearts up to the Father by praying, reading scripture, and receiving Jesus in the Eucharist, we can come to know the love of God intimately.

"Love one another" (John 13:34). Jesus tells us to love others as completely as he loves us. As we accept the love that Jesus has for us, we are empowered to give this same love freely to others. As we give away the love that we have received, we become co-workers with the Spirit, whose mission is to draw the entire world to Jesus. Through our share in divine love, God's life can be magnified and the good news of salvation can go forth.

We are children of God. We are loved far beyond our comprehension. "The LORD is . . . abounding in steadfast love" (Psalm 103:8). He promises to "wipe away every tear" from our eyes (Revelation 21:4). What more could we ask for? What could compare with the experience of God's love being poured into our hearts with all the power of a rushing river? The apostles knew this love and were committed to preaching about Jesus—to the point of laying their lives down for the salvation of others.

It is our love—not our social graces, power, or perfect behavior—that will distinguish us as God's children. We become like Jesus as we love one another with the love that the Spirit pours into us. Let us open ourselves to this call to love so that Jesus' love flows among us—even in the face of rejection and persecution. In all of these things, we become like Jesus, who is the greatest giver of love the world will ever know.

"Lord Jesus, teach us to love others with the same love you have for us. Your love is unconditional, faithful, and full of the promise of new life. May we receive your love through the outpouring of your Holy Spirit, and then do all we can to bring this love to others."

Way, Truth, and Life

JOHN
14:1-31

John 14:1-6

^{1} "Let not your hearts be troubled; believe in God, believe also in me. ^{2} In my Father's house are many rooms; if it were not so, would I have told you that I go to prepare a place for you? ^{3} And when I go and prepare a place for you, I will come again and will take you to myself, that where I am you may be also. ^{4} And you know the way where I am going." ^{5} Thomas said to him, "Lord, we do not know where you are going; how can we know the way?" ^{6} Jesus said to him, "I am the way, and the truth, and the life; no one comes to the Father, but by me."

Having just told them of his imminent betrayal by one of their number, and that Simon Peter—their leader—would deny he ever knew him, Jesus told his disciples, "Let not your hearts be troubled" (John 14:1)! Consider the circumstances: They were living in the tense atmosphere of Roman-occupied Jerusalem. Every day, they faced the threat of imprisonment by the Jewish elders. And, even some of their followers were hoping for a political revolution that would make Jesus king of the new nation of Israel. Now, this Jesus, who had been their spiritual leader—the one they had been following for so long—informs them that he is about to leave them. How could they cope?

The apostles had left everything to follow Jesus. Some members of their families must have begun to wonder about their mental stability. And now they hear that Jesus would be leaving, and worse, that he would be killed. How challenging this must have been to the disciples! But the truth is that Jesus told them this devastating news because he knew that later they would come to understand the fullness of life he was to bring to the world and the absolute necessity of the cross that he was about to embrace.

Jesus came into the world to "destroy the works" of the devil (1 John 3:8). Those who believe in him and are baptized into his name will be saved. We don't have to be perplexed or unduly distressed about the state of the world. We don't have to be bound in anxiety over every aspect of our lives. The joy, peace, and love we long for can be found in Jesus. The way to heaven is not a method or procedure that we must grasp. The way is Jesus himself, who will help us with every step we take in faith. He has redeemed us and established a place in heaven for all who choose to follow him.

This is the Good News. Let us not lose heart. The suffering of the present time is temporary; the joy and glory to come are for all eternity! Whatever you are suffering, God is committed to you. Surrender to God in love and watch him bring good out of even seemingly unbearable situations. Let his Spirit form you more completely into the image of Jesus, who is the fullness of life.

"Lord, we are watching and waiting for your return. Enlighten our minds to preach your word; enkindle our hearts to speak healing words; empower our wills to drive out evil in your name."

John 14:7-14

[7] "If you had known me, you would have known my Father also; henceforth you know him and have seen him."

[8] Philip said to him, "Lord, show us the Father, and we shall be satisfied." [9] Jesus said to him, "Have I been with you so long, and yet you do not know me, Philip? He who has seen me has seen the Father; how can you say, 'Show us the Father'? [10] Do you not believe that I am in the Father and the Father in me? The words that I say to you I do not speak on my own authority; but the Father who dwells in me does his works. [11] Believe me that I am in the Father and the Father in me; or else believe me for the sake of the works themselves.

[12] "Truly, truly, I say to you, he who believes in me will also do the works that I do; and greater works than these will he do, because I go to the Father. [13] Whatever you ask in my name, I will do it, that the Father may be glorified in the Son; [14] if you ask anything in my name, I will do it."

In response to Philip's request to see the Father, Jesus challenged him, and all the disciples, to believe in the special relationship between the Father and the Son. He wanted to teach them that living faith—belief in Christ—would open them up to the truth of who he is, and that as they came to understand more of Jesus, they would also understand the Father more fully.

At different points in his ministry, Jesus told his listeners that he spoke under and with the Father's authority—even that he himself was God (John 12:49-50; 14:11). Among the many aspects of Jesus' mission was to reveal the Father (14:8-10), "to bear witness to the truth" (18:37), and to give his followers the "power to become children of God" (1:12). All this so that we might share in the eternal union between the Father and the Son (17:20-24).

To glorify the Father, Jesus promised the disciples that after his resurrection and return to the Father, he would grant whatever they asked in his name (John 14:12-13; 15:16). He even promised the disciples that if they believed in him they would do greater works than he. Since his disciples do the same works as Jesus—glorifying the Father by bringing all people back into union with the Father and the Son—Jesus will do what they ask in his name. Thus the disciples, like Jesus, would ultimately be doing the Father's work.

Jesus' promise to his first disciples is just as true for us. By believing in the risen Lord, we become participants in the union between the Father and Son. Therefore, whatever we ask in Jesus' name he will do. As we listen to Jesus, we accomplish the work of the Father and glorify both the Father and the Son. Every act of love, service, and humility done in the name of the Lord brings great glory to Jesus and advances his kingdom in the hearts of his people. Every time we turn away from sin in repentance, share the good news with someone, or choose to obey God rather than our fallen desires, the Father is glorified and the world receives yet another witness of the power of the gospel. We can do mighty works in the name of the Lord because Christ is in us and longs to work through us.

Nothing we do is inconsequential. Our actions have eternal significance. We are called, just as Jesus was, to accomplish the Father's work in the world by proclaiming the good news and advancing God's kingdom. Let us commit ourselves to glorifying the Father in everything we do. Let us commit ourselves to believing in Jesus with our whole hearts so that the world may come to believe in him as well.

"Lord Jesus, I rejoice in your resurrection, through which I have been brought into union with you and with the Father. In your name I pray that the Father's work will be accomplished through me."

John 14:15-21

[15] "If you love me, you will keep my commandments. [16] And I will pray the Father, and he will give you another Counselor, to be with you for ever, [17] even the Spirit of truth, whom the world cannot receive, because it neither sees him nor knows him; you know him, for he dwells with you, and will be in you.
[18] "I will not leave you desolate; I will come to you. [19] Yet a little while, and the world will see me no more, but you will see me; because I live, you will live also. [20] In that day you will know that I am in my Father, and you in me, and I in you. [21] He who has my commandments and keeps them, he it is who loves me; and he who loves me will be loved by my Father, and I will love him and manifest myself to him."

As Christians, we can be tempted to feel scattered and isolated in the midst of a culture that does not share our faith and hope in Christ. This must be how Peter felt at the Last Supper, as Jesus explained his mission and the promises that would be fulfilled through his cross. Years later, Peter addressed a pastoral letter "to the exiles of the Dispersion" (1 Peter 1:1). Such a description of what it means to be a disciple of Jesus can encourage us and teach us how to live our faith: "In your hearts reverence Christ as Lord" (1 Peter 3:15).

Jesus alone is able to secure for us the Father's blessing and the consolation of the Spirit. We can place all our confidence in him. We are called to set apart Christ in our hearts because he has taken up residence in us through his Spirit (John 14:17). When we set him apart as Lord, we are saying that we recognize the gift that has been given to us and that we want to decrease while Christ who is in us rules us more and more (3:30).

On the eve of his death, Jesus told his disciples, "He who has my commandments and keeps them, he it is who loves me" (John 14:21). This obedience does not consist merely in adhering to a set of rules. Rather, Christ himself is our rule of life, and his words come to life in our hearts through the indwelling Holy Spirit. Moved by his love, we show our love for Jesus by obeying his voice rather than listening to the objections, fears, and self-directed voices of the fallen nature in us.

Listen to how St. Bernard of Clairvaux described this interior movement of the Spirit in his life:

> I understood that he was there due to certain movements in my own heart: The fleeing of the vices and the repression of my carnal appetites has made known to me the strength of his virtue. . . . Even the slightest amendment of my way of life has given me the experience of this sweet bounty; seeking the renewal and reformation of my mind, that is, the interior man in me, I have perceived something of his beauty; finally, contemplating the wonder of his greatness in all this has left me speechless. (*On the Song of Songs*, Sermon 74.6)

The more we venerate the Spirit in our hearts, the more deeply he can lead us to the truth, and greater will be our ability to know Christ and to live in his way.

John 14:22-26

²² Judas (not Iscariot) said to him, "Lord, how is it that you will manifest yourself to us, and not to the world?" ²³ Jesus answered him, "If a man loves me, he will keep my word, and my Father will love him, and we will come to him and make our home with him. ²⁴ He who does not love me does not keep my words; and the word which you hear is not mine but the Father's who sent me. ²⁵ "These things I have spoken to you, while I am still with you. ²⁶ But the Counselor, the Holy Spirit, whom the Father will send in my name, he will teach you all things, and bring to your remembrance all that I have said to you."

Jesus knew that his announcement that he was leaving them would trouble his disciples. He also knew, however, that their love for him would overcome their fear and give way to joy. They would not be left alone; the Holy Spirit would be sent by the Father to teach them all things and remind them of everything that Jesus had revealed to them (John 14:26).

Jesus called his disciples to enter into the love that he and his Father shared: "If anyone loves me, he will keep my word, and my Father will love him, and we will come to him and make our home with him" (John 14:23). What a powerful promise! We are meant to be a "home" for Almighty God! God wants to live within us and, through us, to touch the world with his love and mercy. Time and again, through the prophets of the Old Testament, he called his people back to love and follow him as their Father; now he gives us that same commission. It is our obedience to God's commands that will open the door of God's blessings and enable us to fulfill this prophetic calling.

We may ask how we can hope to remain obedient when temptation can be so strong. But this is the very reason why God poured out his Spirit. The Spirit has been given to teach us about the Father's love and to reveal the power of Jesus' resurrection in our lives. As we open ourselves to his teaching, our relationship with God will deepen and we will be conformed to his likeness. We will learn to turn to God more quickly during times of temptation. We will become wiser in our dealings with other people. We will trust that the power of the indwelling Spirit is greater than any other power that might stand against us. In short, we will become more and more like Jesus.

How often have we observed the similarities between a father and son, a daughter and a mother? Mannerisms, speech, even the way they walk are often very similar. It is the daily contact and the intimacy of a family that makes this happen. It is the same with God. The more time we spend with him, the more we will become like him. Let us embrace the power of the resurrection within us and ask the Spirit to continue to conform us to the likeness of Christ.

"Holy Spirit, bring Jesus' promises to life in my heart today. Help me to believe and to have hope that the Father's love will dwell richly in my heart. May your presence within me become my guiding light, and may your love shine out to everyone I meet today."

John 14:27-31

27 "Peace I leave with you; my peace I give to you; not as the world gives do I give to you. Let not your hearts be troubled, neither let them be afraid. 28 You heard me say to you, 'I go away, and I will come to you.' If you loved me, you would have rejoiced, because I go to the Father; for the Father is greater than I. 29 And now I have told you before it takes place, so that when it does take place, you may believe. 30 I will no longer talk much with you, for the ruler of this world is coming. He has no power over me; 31 but I do as the Father has commanded me, so that the world may know that I love the Father. Rise, let us go hence."

Peace I leave with you. (John 14:27)

Throughout Jesus' time on earth, he revealed the peace of God—a peace that surpasses all understanding. At the outset of his ministry, Jesus was led by the Spirit into the desert where he was subjected to profound temptations by Satan. Yet even in the face of these demonic attacks, Jesus held firm to the love and truth of his Father (Luke 4:1-13).

Often, Jesus would go to a quiet place to pray and listen to God. During these special times, he would eagerly receive the grace and peace that God lavished upon him. In the boat with the apostles, when a terrible storm developed, Jesus remained asleep in the stern, unperturbed by the turmoil (Luke 8:22-25). When he was awakened by the frantic apostles, he rebuked the wind and reminded them of their Father's all-surpassing dominion and care.

Wherever Jesus went, crowds pressed in to receive healing and deliverance, yet he never felt overwhelmed. Rather, he turned continually to the Father, relying on his wisdom and strength. Because Jesus responded to each situation only as the Father directed him to, he was able to remain in the peace of God and to minister that peace to everyone who sought him out.

Jesus' heart was grounded in love for his Father, trust in him, and complete reliance on his power. Even as he imparted his peace to his disciples, he knew that his time to take up the cross was drawing near. Still, he declared his Father's greatness: "The Father is greater than I" (John 14:28); "I go to the Father" (14:28); "I love the Father" (14:31). Nothing, not even the cross, could disrupt his peace and confidence in God.

We all face trials, disappointments, and fears. And, in each of these situations, Jesus says, "Peace I leave with you. My peace I give to you" (John 14:27). Even during times when we are not beset by troubles, Jesus continues to speak these words to us. He wants to fill our hearts always with his abiding presence. He longs to draw us to the Father's side so that we can know the kind of peace that does not depend on the situations around us, but on the steadfast, solid love of God.

"Jesus, Prince of Peace, come reign in my heart! Remind me of the Father's perfect love and mercy. Holy Spirit, strengthen my trust in the Father so that I would walk each day in the peace and presence of the Trinity."

The True Vine

John 15:1-8

[1] "I am the true vine, and my Father is the vinedresser. [2] Every branch of mine that bears no fruit, he takes away, and every branch that does bear fruit he prunes, that it may bear more fruit. [3] You are already made clean by the word which I have spoken to you. [4] Abide in me, and I in you. As the branch cannot bear fruit by itself, unless it abides in the vine, neither can you, unless you abide in me. [5] I am the vine, you are the branches. He who abides in me, and I in him, he it is that bears much fruit, for apart from me you can do nothing. [6] If a man does not abide in me, he is cast forth as a branch and withers; and the branches are gathered, thrown into the fire and burned. [7] If you abide in me, and my words abide in you, ask whatever you will, and it shall be done for you. [8] By this my Father is glorified, that you bear much fruit, and so prove to be my disciples."

In the Old Testament, Israel is often compared to a vine. Speaking symbolically, many prophets spoke of how God planted and took care of the vine, but the vine went bad and was ultimately trampled under foot: "I planted you a choice vine, wholly of pure seed. How then have you turned degenerate and become a wild vine?" (Jeremiah 2:21; see also Isaiah 5:1-7; Ezekiel 19:10-14; Psalm 80:8-15).

Following in this tradition, Jesus told his disciples, "I am the true vine, and my Father is the vine-dresser" (John 15:1). The promise was clear: In Jesus and his followers, the Father will find the kind of fruit he desires. Our job is to remain connected to the vine, drawing our nourishment from Christ. It is our Father's job to tend the vine and bring it to full fruitfulness. This statement sounds so explicit that we could miss the greatness of its challenge and promise.

In following Jesus, our tendency is to preempt God's work by taking the pruning shears into our own hands—to replace his divine work with something of our own making. We design self-help projects that tend to focus on shortcomings in our lives that we are embarrassed about. But this will never help us get to the deeper kinds of heart changes that God wants to work in us. These are the changes we need if we want to experience new life because they are the fruit of God's action and our cooperation, not our action alone.

When God works in someone's life, that person shines like a star in the midst of a darkened world (Philippians 2:15). We may sometimes face trials and difficulties in our lives caused by our attachments to things that are not of God. But when we submit these things to the hand of God, our ungodly attachments can be pruned away so that we can bear fruit. No self-help project, no amount of study or devotions can compare with God's gentle pruning touch.

Jesus promised that the Father himself would prune the vine and make us fruitful, for he is the vine-dresser. A tremendous sense of security is ours when we recognize this truth. Who could be more dependable, more patient, more loving, and more desirous of our growth than our heavenly Father? How could we not submit the desires of our heart to him?

"Father, cut away from me the tendrils of my worldly attachments and strengthen me to yield a rich and abundant harvest for your kingdom."

John 15:9-11

9 "As the Father has loved me, so have I loved you; abide in my love. 10 If you keep my commandments, you will abide in my love, just as I have kept my Father's commandments and abide in his love. 11 These things I have spoken to you, that my joy may be in you, and that your joy may be full."

As the Father has loved me, so have I loved you. (John 15:9)

The miracle of love is that God himself is love. Love is not something he says or does—it is the very essence of who he is. All the other characteristics of God are but extensions of his love. God is all-knowing, all-powerful, just, and merciful, because he is love.

To grasp the love that God has for us, it is essential to understand that love the Father has for his Son, for it is the same love. God's love for his Son is eternal; it neither began with the incarnation of Christ nor ended with his resurrection. Jesus was with the Father from the beginning and is the first object of his love (John 1:1-2; 17:24). Therefore, when Jesus tells us he loves us just as the Father loves him, it is not restricted to space and time; it is as everlasting as God himself.

Jesus loves us with a love that gives everything it possesses and keeps nothing for itself. The Father and the Son are one in that love. All that the Father is and has, he has given to Jesus. As with the Father, Jesus gave himself totally for the sake of love. He did not consider even his life or his body too much to give for us (John 3:16-17). And in a manner that surpasses understanding, he made himself one with his church, the body of Christ. He will never leave us. He will never abandon his church.

Jesus loves us with a tender, covenant love. He is not deterred by our sins and failings because his love is greater than our fickle hearts (1 John 3:19-20). He envelops our fallibility, our slow growth, and our many fears with gentle compassion and continues to work in our hearts (Psalm 73:26). He is fully committed to us and will never stop offering us opportunities to grow closer to him and receive his love more fully.

When the love of Jesus touches our hearts, it melts the hardness and produces in us a love for him. We begin to long for him so much that we want to obey his commandments because we know that obedience to his word will further our growth in the knowledge of his love (John 15:10). We begin to see with spiritual eyes that his will and his ways are far greater than our ideas and wishes.

Catherine of Siena described it well when she wrote:

"You are love itself. So the soul who follows your Truth's teaching in love becomes through love another you. Dispossessed of her own will, she is so well clothed in yours that she neither seeks nor desires anything but what you seek and will for her." (*Prayers*, 11)

John 15:12-17

[12] "This is my commandment, that you love one another as I have loved you. [13] Greater love has no man than this, that a man lay down his life for his friends. [14] You are my friends if you do what I command you. [15] No longer do I call you servants, for the servant

does not know what his master is doing; but I have called you friends, for all that I have heard from my Father I have made known to you. [16] You did not choose me, but I chose you and appointed you that you should go and bear fruit and that your fruit should abide; so that whatever you ask the Father in my name, he may give it to you. [17] This I command you, to love one another."

Friends of Jesus Christ—what an honor! We have not taken such a title upon ourselves, but have received it from God. Jesus loves each one of us with love unsurpassed by any we know. "Greater love has no man than this, that a man lay down his life for his friends" (John 15:13). Because this is what Jesus did for us, we can be completely confident that we are his friends.

Jesus is the ultimate friend. No love is greater than the love he offers. This is not an abstract love, but a divine affection that we can experience. He demonstrates his love for us in concrete, discernible ways. The most powerful, of course, was his willingness to die for us. But every day, he offers us gifts: patience when irritability threatens to cause riot in our souls; gentleness when violence seeks to rage in us; wisdom when we are at our wits' end. And always there is the gift of salvation—our forgiveness, rebirth, and the promise of everlasting life!

As the Spirit writes the word "friend" on our hearts, we begin to taste Jesus' love for us. Condemnation comes to an end. Fear, guilt, and anxiety are replaced with forgiveness, contentment, and peace. The assurance that we are well cared for drives out discouragement and doubt. Our lives take on a greater purpose as we respond to Jesus' call to be a light to the world and salt for the earth (Matthew 5:13-16). Everything that Jesus received from his Father finds a home in our spirits, and we begin to bear fruit (John 15:16).

Every day, many times a day, Jesus offers us practical proofs of his love and friendship. Not for ourselves only—not to be amassed in some kind of spiritual hoard—but so that we would be enabled to love others as we are loved. In this way, we fulfill Jesus' command to love one another and so are conformed to Jesus' image (John 15:12). This is what Jesus intended for his church.

"Lord Jesus, thank you for choosing me as your friend. I rejoice in your friendship and in the transformation that your Spirit brings about in my life. I commit myself to you, to serve you, and to obey you as long as I live."

John 15:18-25

18 "If the world hates you, know that it has hated me before it hated you. 19 If you were of the world, the world would love its own; but because you are not of the world, but I chose you out of the world, therefore the world hates you. 20 Remember the word that I said to you, 'A servant is not greater than his master.' If they persecuted me, they will persecute you; if they kept my word, they will keep yours also. 21 But all this they will do to you on my account, because they do not know him who sent me. 22 If I had not come and spoken to them, they would not have sin; but now they have no excuse for their sin. 23 He who hates me hates my Father also. 24 If I had not done among them the works which no one else did, they would not have sin; but now they have seen and hated both me and my Father. 25 It is to fulfill the word that is written in their law, 'They hated me without a cause.' "

If the world hates you, know that it has hated me
before it hated you. (John 15:18)

W hen Jesus spoke of the "world," he was not alluding to the
natural universe, but to fallen humanity. In Johannine
writing, the "world" represented an evil system, controlled
by the forces of darkness. Everything in it was opposed to the reign
of God. That's why Jesus told his disciples in strong terms, "Because
you are not of the world . . . the world hates you" (John 15:19). This
hatred was experienced by Jesus firsthand and he warned his followers: "A servant is not greater than his master. If they persecuted
me, they will persecute you" (15:20). His prophecy has been proved
true in every age through the lives of the saints.

John Bosco (1815-1888) was a priest and teacher renowned
throughout Italy for his work with poor children and orphans. Yet
his kindness and generosity did not spare him from persecution.
Italian politics in his day was strongly anti-Catholic, and Bosco was
often vilified in the press. He survived several vicious physical attacks
from hired thugs. Once, an assassin's bullet passed right through his
loose cloak, barely missing him. However, it was said that the gentle Don Bosco never let adversity destroy his cheerful demeanor in
the service of Christ.

The Polish Franciscan Maximilian Kolbe (1894-1941) faced perhaps the most systematic form of evil of the twentieth century. He
courageously denounced Nazism in the years before World War II.
When Nazi troops conquered Poland, they imprisoned Kolbe in the
Auschwitz concentration camp. Eyewitnesses testify that the guards
frequently abused the frail priest, but could never destroy his inner
peace or prevent him from helping fellow prisoners. So great was his
love for Christ that Kolbe voluntarily took the place of another pris-
oner who had been condemned to death. The Nazis executed this
resolute Christian on August 14, 1941.

The Son of God entered the world precisely because it was a place of great darkness. He came to deliver all those who, held in the grip of evil, knew nothing of God's love: "They do not know him who sent me" (John 15:21). Jesus calls his followers out of the world to become lights in the darkness. In doing so, he promises that they will endure persecution, but he also pledges that they will witness love conquering hatred, and life triumphing over death. By imitating Christ's self-sacrifice, Christians serve as a living sacrament, a sign that the Lord of life is truly risen and has overcome the darkness of this world.

John 15:26–16:4

26 "But when the Counselor comes, whom I shall send to you from the Father, even the Spirit of truth, who proceeds from the Father, he will bear witness to me; 27 and you also are witnesses, because you have been with me from the beginning.
16:1 "I have said all this to you to keep you from falling away.
2 They will put you out of the synagogues; indeed, the hour is coming when whoever kills you will think he is offering service to God. 3 And they will do this because they have not known the Father, nor me. 4 But I have said these things to you, that when their hour comes you may remember that I told you of them. I did not say these things to you from the beginning, because I was with you."

I did not say these things to you from the beginning, because I was with you.
(John 16:4)

The lot of the first Christians was not an easy one. Most were Jews who had embraced Jesus as the Messiah and as a result were persecuted. To be "put out of the synagogue" meant that the Jewish leaders barred Christians from worship and fellowship with other Jews (John 9:22,34; 16:2). Considering how community-minded first-century Jews were, we can appreciate some of the pain and sadness that these first believers must have experienced.

But Jesus promised his disciples the Spirit, who would continue to reveal to them Jesus' love and protection (John 15:26). It was by the Spirit's power that these first Christians endured hardship and persecution calmly and heroically. The *Letter to Diognetus*, an ancient, anonymous Christian epistle, describes the early believers' hearts and their ability to remain steadfast in the face of misunderstanding and persecution:

> Christians love all men; but all men persecute them. Condemned because they are not understood, they are put to death, but raised to life again. They live in poverty; but enrich many. They are totally destitute; but possess an abundance of everything. They suffer dishonor; but that is their glory. They are defamed, but vindicated. A blessing is their answer to abuse, deference their response to insult. For the good they do they receive the punishment of malefactors, but even then they rejoice, as though receiving the gift of life.

It is easy to forget that persecution continues today. All over the world, we have brothers and sisters in Christ who suffer

because of their love for the Lord. Some are tortured and even martyred by anti-Christian guerrilla groups; others are cast out of their
families and clans. Still more suffer when their obedience to the
truth conflicts with the expectations of family or peers. Yet their
witness continues, and the gospel advances.

Jesus was right: Those who follow him can expect hardship and
trials as they live the good news. But Jesus also promised that the
Holy Spirit would be with us to strengthen and comfort us. We are
not alone; God's love within us and between us is a source of great
joy, a joy that overcomes difficulty.

"Holy Spirit, be my strength and joy as I witness to Jesus. I pray
also for all who are persecuted for their witness to Christ. Comfort
them today. Protect and encourage them. Build your church on the
witness of their faith."

The Promise of the Spirit

JOHN
16:5-33

John 16:5-11

⁵ "But now I am going to him who sent me; yet none of you asks me, 'Where are you going?' ⁶ But because I have said these things to you, sorrow has filled your hearts. ⁷ Nevertheless I tell you the truth: it is to your advantage that I go away, for if I do not go away, the Counselor will not come to you; but if I go, I will send him to you. ⁸ And when he comes, he will convince the world concerning sin and righteousness and judgment: ⁹ concerning sin, because they do not believe in me; ¹⁰ concerning righteousness, because I go to the Father, and you will see me no more; ¹¹ concerning judgment, because the ruler of this world is judged."

Jesus understood something his disciples did not yet comprehend: He had to return to the Father so that the Paraclete could be poured out (John 16:5,7). When the Spirit came, their hearts and minds would be transformed and their vision of the heavenly life sharpened. Reflecting on Jesus' departure and the coming of the Spirit, St. Cyril of Alexandria (d. 444) wrote:

With the resurrection, the earthly work of Jesus was complete, but men and women still had to become sharers in the Word's divine nature. Our present mode of life had to be put aside and we had to be transformed into new beings with a new way of existing. This change could not take place if we did not share in the Holy Spirit. (*Commentary on John's Gospel*)

This inner transformation would take place in a threefold way. First, the Spirit would convince the world about sin and not believing in Jesus (John 16:9). Second, the Spirit would show how Jesus' resurrection and ascension proved him righteous and cleared him of the charges against him (16:10). Finally, the Spirit would prove to the world that Jesus defeated sin and Satan by his death on the cross and freed humanity from bondage to sin (16:11).

The Spirit came to do a heavenly work—to convince the world about heavenly realities. Through the Spirit, God wants to restore us to fullness in him. He didn't send the Spirit just to fix us up a little, but that is often all we seek. Sometimes we can be quite happy with a little revelation from the Spirit or with a few sin patterns healed, but we're not sure whether we want the full work of restoration that the Holy Spirit wants to effect in us.

It would be helpful to ask ourselves some questions: How much am I willing to allow God to touch my life? Do I want him to restore me fully to himself, or am I satisfied with some minor improvements? Do I fear that if I let the Spirit do too much, I won't end up happy or fulfilled? Can I trust that he only wants to deliver me from sin so that he can fill me with love and peace?

The Spirit will transform us. According to St. Cyril, "He shifts their attention from earthly things to heavenly things, and makes timid and weak souls strong and generous." In this, "the disciples were certainly so changed that no persecution could daunt them, and they devoted themselves to Christ with wholehearted love." Such is the change that will take place in us if we invite the Holy Spirit into our lives and desire the fullness of his presence.

John 16:12-15

[12] "I have yet many things to say to you, but you cannot bear them now. [13] When the Spirit of truth comes, he will guide you into all the truth; for he will not speak on his own authority, but whatever he hears he will speak, and he will declare to you the things that are to come. [14] He will glorify me, for he will take what is mine and declare it to you. [15] All that the Father has is mine; therefore I said that he will take what is mine and declare it to you."

When the Spirit of truth comes,
he will guide you into all the truth. (John 16:13)

Have you ever noticed how difficult it can be at times to determine the truth in a given situation? We are barraged with conflicting choices in everything from choosing a shampoo to raising children. Every alternative set before us claims to be the best way, and we find ourselves pulled in so many directions that we lose sight of what we started out to do. God knows our every need and has made provision to lead us from confusion into clarity through the gift of his Holy Spirit. Through the action of the Spirit, we can separate wheat from chaff, truth from deception, and choose life instead of death.

What characterizes the Spirit of truth and what are the truths he addresses? To begin, the Spirit gives us knowledge that leads us to praise God the Father and Jesus his Son. He is our Counselor and our teacher (John 14:26). He intercedes for us when we ourselves do not even know how to pray (Romans 8:26). The Spirit leads us to truth in every situation—spiritual and physical—if we but listen to him. He leads us to recognize that each of us is a participant in the fall of man. None of us is sinless. The Holy Spirit teaches us about the righteousness of Jesus, his sinless nature, and his action in saving us from everlasting separation from God.

Through the Spirit, we come to accept the forgiveness that God has given us through his Son. Lastly, we come to know that Satan and his power have been defeated and that judgment will come for each of us (John 16:8-11). In all things, the Spirit leads us to a deeper knowledge of Jesus as "the way, and the truth, and the life" (14:6).

In all these ways, the Spirit guides us into the truth. But greater even than all this, the Spirit brings us to a personal, ongoing encounter with Jesus Christ, who is truth incarnate. He fills our hearts with the love and presence of Jesus, and in the light of the love of the Lord, we begin to think differently about our lives and about the world around us. We long for heaven. We burn to share the gospel. We are filled with compassion and are moved to feed the hungry, clothe the naked, and care for the ailing. Through the Spirit's continuing work in our lives, we are set free to "become partakers of the divine nature" (2 Peter 1:4), and our hearts are inflamed with the hope that we will one day be fully incorporated into the life and love of Jesus, our hope.

"Holy Spirit, work in my life in a new way. Teach me about the kingdom of God. Show me my need for Jesus. Reveal to me the love of Christ and lead me according to his will. Give me the desire and the strength to serve the body of Christ and to share this new life with those I meet."

John 16:16-22

¹⁶ "A little while, and you will see me no more; again a little while, and you will see me." ¹⁷ Some of his disciples said to one another, "What is this that he says to us, 'A little while, and you will not see me, and again a little while, and you will see me'; and, 'because I go to the Father'?" ¹⁸ They said, "What does he mean by 'a little while'? We do not know what he means." ¹⁹ Jesus knew that they wanted to ask him; so he said to them, "Is this what you are asking yourselves, what I meant by saying, 'A little while, and you will not see me, and again a little while, and you will see me'? ²⁰ Truly, truly, I say to you, you will weep and lament, but the world will rejoice; you will be sorrowful, but your sorrow will turn into joy. ²¹ When a woman is in travail she has sorrow, because her hour has come; but when she is delivered of the child, she no longer remembers the anguish, for joy that a child is born into the world. ²² So you have sorrow now, but I will see you again and your hearts will rejoice, and no one will take your joy from you."

You will be sorrowful, but your sorrow will turn into joy" (John 16:20). "Rejoice in the Lord always; again I will say, Rejoice" (Philippians 4:4). "Though you do not see him, you believe in him and rejoice with unutterable and exalted joy" (1 Peter 1:8). What is this "joy" that is such a common word in the scriptures?

Jesus told his disciples that they would first experience sorrow while the world rejoiced, but that their sorrow would turn to joy (John 16:20). This sorrow and joy centered around the fact that Jesus had to leave them in order to send the Holy Spirit. The disciples would grieve at the departure of their Savior, but their grief would become joy when the Holy Spirit came into their hearts.

This quality of joy comes about as a result of the work of God in us. It goes deeper than the fleeting emotions we know all too well, for its origin is the Holy Spirit, whose love and peace are eternal. In other parts of John's Gospel, Jesus promised his disciples (and us) that he would make their joy full and complete (John 15:11; 16:24). This is not to say that we will never experience further joy, such as at the second coming of Christ. Rather, our joy even now can be full because Jesus, the object of our joy, is being revealed to us by the power of the Holy Spirit.

Because this joy comes from the Spirit, and because it is based on the eternal love of God, no one can take it from us (John 16:22). The only way we can lose our joy is by neglecting prayer, ignoring repentance, and growing lax in our devotion to scripture. As we remain faithful in these areas, we allow the Holy Spirit to produce the life of the Trinity within us, and in this life is contained the fullness of joy because it is a life of intimate closeness with a God whose love and provision for us never end. It is a life of joy because it places us in touch with a Father who delights in blessing us, a Father whose loving gaze is always fixed on us.

"Heavenly Father, you sent your Spirit to reveal the glory of Jesus Christ to all who would believe in him. Teach me to rejoice in the Spirit's coming. May I hunger for his presence within me and seek him out in prayer and your word. Lord Jesus, increase my faith in your death and resurrection so I may rejoice in the new life that you have gained for me."

John 16:23-28

²³ "In that day you will ask nothing of me. Truly, truly, I say to you, if you ask anything of the Father, he will give it to you in my name. ²⁴ Hitherto you have asked nothing in my name; ask, and you will receive, that your joy may be full.

²⁵ "I have said this to you in figures; the hour is coming when I shall no longer speak to you in figures but tell you plainly of the Father. ²⁶ In that day you will ask in my name; and I do not say to you that I shall pray the Father for you; ²⁷ for the Father himself loves you, because you have loved me and have believed that I came from the Father. ²⁸ I came from the Father and have come into the world; again, I am leaving the world and going to the Father."

Near the end of his last intimate talk with his disciples before his death, Jesus reminded them that "in that day" of the coming of the Spirit, they would be able to overcome the fear and confusion caused by his passion, death, and resurrection and witness to their significance. He reassured them of the Father's love and further promised: "If you ask anything of the Father, he will give it to you in my name" (John 16:23). He promised them that, because they loved and believed in him, they would experience the fullness of the Father's love.

This promise of the Father's love is still available to us today. If we love and obey Jesus, we will be empowered to lead new lives under the anointing of the Holy Spirit. All too often we want love but reject obedience. We want to receive the gifts of the Spirit and the fruit of the Spirit, but we want them while living quite independently of God's will for our lives.

St. John of Avila (1500-1569), commenting on the indwelling Holy Spirit, said: "He who desires the Holy Spirit, let him love and obey and desire Jesus Christ forever! . . . There are no better chains with which to hold the Holy Spirit than by loving Jesus Christ" (*Sermons*, Pentecost Sunday). Jesus himself has told us that loving is not merely a matter of saying "Lord, Lord!" (Matthew 7:21); it requires acknowledging God's sovereignty by obeying his will and commands (John 14:15; 15:10).

Obedience to God involves making decisions according to God's commandments rather than according to the demands of our fallen nature. It means coming daily before the Father in prayer, repenting for our unbelief and disobedience, and believing that God will speak to us through his Spirit. It means reading scripture as a way of allowing God to make known how he wants us to live as his sons and daughters.

Commitment to Jesus and to the right use of the gifts of the Spirit will bring us new life—life filled with the blessings promised to us by the Father. John of Avila further counseled in this regard: "Think about Jesus Christ! Obey him; love him from the depths of your heart so that the Holy Spirit may come to you." Let's invite the Spirit into our hearts every day as we humbly seek to obey the word of the Lord.

John 16:29-33

[29] His disciples said, "Ah, now you are speaking plainly, not in any figure! [30] Now we know that you know all things, and need none to question you; by this we believe that you came from God." [31] Jesus answered them, "Do you now believe? [32] The hour is coming, indeed it has come, when you will be scattered, every man to his home, and will leave me alone; yet I am not alone, for the Father is with me. [33] I have said this to you, that in me you may have peace. In the world you have tribulation; but be of good cheer, I have overcome the world."

In the world you have tribulation; but be of good cheer,
I have overcome the world. (John 16:33)

The early disciples faced fearsome tribulations: rejection by their own people, persecution, imprisonment, even martyrdom (2 Corinthians 6:3-10). Yet even in the midst of their trials, they never lost their trust in God or their love for him. Most probably, our own afflictions are not as severe as those of the early disciples—painful as they may sometimes seem to us.

For us, trials usually mean deciding to do what is right despite the temptation to take an easier way out. This could mean adopting an unpopular position on a family, political, or social issue and enduring criticism as a result. It could mean sacrificing our free time and comfort to serve the poor and needy. It might mean working with our children to teach them to love and obey the Lord, even though our initial efforts may have aroused resistance and hostility.

Our difficulties may differ in nature from those of the early disciples, but the peace they experienced is the same peace that can be ours. Jesus encourages all of us to "be of good cheer" (John 16:33). The original Greek word for cheer, *tharseo*, meant more than just having a pleasant disposition or always looking happy. It was a call to have courage and confidence. We can take heart in the midst of tribulation—we can be courageous and confident—because Jesus has won victory over the world. Through our baptism into Christ, we have been given a share in his resurrection life. We can set our minds on the things of heaven; the problems we face in the world do not have to overwhelm us (Colossians 3:1-4).

As we take this position of victory in Christ, we can have new minds and new attitudes about our trials. When we allow our minds and hearts to be formed by the word of God, we can look upon the world in the same way that God does. Our situations can be viewed more objectively, and we can walk in confidence and obedience. God would never ask us to face anything that he had not provided the grace to handle (1 Corinthians 10:13). Knowing that Jesus has overcome the world and given us a share in his victory, we can rise above every situation.

"Jesus, you gave your disciples victory over every trial. By your Spirit, give me that same faith and confidence. Help me to take heart and be confident in you."

Jesus' Final Prayer

JOHN
17:1-26

John 17:1-10

[1] When Jesus had spoken these words, he lifted up his eyes to heaven and said, "Father, the hour has come; glorify your Son that the Son may glorify you, [2] since you have given him power over all flesh, to give eternal life to all whom you have given him. [3] And this is eternal life, that they know you the only true God, and Jesus Christ whom you have sent. [4] I glorified you on earth, having accomplished the work which you gave me to do; [5] and now, Father, glorify me in your own presence with the glory which I had with you before the world was made.

[6] "I have manifested your name to the men whom you gave me out of the world; yours they were, and you gave them to me, and they have kept your word [7] Now they know that everything that you have given me is from you; [8] for I have given them the words which you gave me, and they have received them and know in truth that I came from you; and they have believed that you did send me. [9] I am praying for them; I am not praying for the world but for those whom you have given me, for they are yours; [10] all mine are yours, and yours are mine, and I am glorified in them."

Several significant discourses in the Gospel of John take place between the Last Supper and Jesus' trial and death. In one of these, often called the high priestly prayer, Jesus declared, "The hour has come" (John 17:1). What was this hour? Elsewhere, scripture refers to Jesus' betrayal by Judas as the "hour of darkness" (Mark 14:41; Luke 22:53), but in John's theology, it was the hour of Jesus' glory: "Father, the hour has come; glorify your Son so that the Son may glorify you" (John 17:1).

Jesus anticipated this hour constantly. At various times, starting with the wedding at Cana, he said that his hour had not yet come (John 2:4; 7:30; 8:20). With his triumphant entry into Jerusalem, however, he announced, "The hour has come for the Son of man to be glorified" (12:23). And later, John tells us, "Jesus knew that his hour had come to . . . go to the Father" (13:1).

Knowing his enemies were about to seize him, Jesus trusted in his Father's plan of salvation. He knew—as John's symbolism portrays—that his crucifixion and his glorification were one and the same event. On the cross, Jesus was "lifted up from the earth" (John 12:32), that is, exalted. In his passion, death, and resurrection, he assumed the lordship intended for him since the moment of his incarnation.

In this priestly prayer, Jesus also declared to his Father, "You have given [me] authority over all people, to give eternal life to all whom you have given [me]" (John 17:2). That authority came through Jesus' ultimate act of obedience: "I glorified you on earth by finishing the work that you gave me to do" (17:4). Now the Father would glorify his Son by giving him the name above all other names, supreme authority over all of creation. Knowing what it meant, Jesus embraced his hour and prayed, "So now, Father, glorify me in your own presence with the glory that I had in your presence before the world existed" (17:5).

We should reflect on John's sense of how deeply and intricately Jesus' suffering is related to his glorification. As we spend time pondering this truth in scripture, we can be sure that the Holy Spirit will enlighten us. The Spirit delights in giving his people a profound knowledge of salvation. Our worship in private prayer and in the liturgy, which recalls that "hour," will deepen. So will our faith in God's tremendous plan for our salvation. Let us ask the Holy Spirit to give us the mind of Christ.

John 17:11-19

[11] "And now I am no more in the world, but they are in the world, and I am coming to you. Holy Father, keep them in your name, which you have given me, that they may be one, even as we are one. [12] While I was with them, I kept them in your name, which you have given me; I have guarded them, and none of them is lost but the son of perdition, that the scripture might be fulfilled. [13] But now I am coming to you; and these things I speak in the world, that they may have my joy fulfilled in themselves. [14] I have given them your word; and the world has hated them because they are not of the world, even as I am not of the world. [15] I do not pray that you should take them out of the world, but that you should keep them from the evil one. [16] They are not of the world, even as I am not of the world. [17] Sanctify them in the truth; your word is truth. [18] As you did send me into the world, so I have sent them into the world. [19] And for their sake I consecrate myself, that they also may be consecrated in truth."

Jesus prayed to his Father for his disciples, "Sanctify them in the truth; your word is truth" (John 17:17). To be sanctified in the truth means to be set apart by inner acceptance of the truth, to obey it, and so to be made holy for God's purposes. Throughout his gospel, John goes to great lengths to portray Jesus as the Word of God who sanctifies his people in the truth by word and sacrament.

Being sanctified in the truth by the word has to do with receiving, obeying, and living out the word of God. It involves allowing our minds to be made one with the mind of God as we read scrip-

ture and beg the Holy Spirit to bring it to life for us. It means taking on the mind of Christ in the course of the day by asking the Spirit
to prompt us and help us examine our consciences. Just as Jesus' mind
and will were one with the Father's, so can ours be one with his.

Through sacrament too we are able to experience a close
union with God and his holiness. As we receive the body and blood
of Christ, God's life in us can transform us, strengthen us, and heal
us. When we receive Jesus with an active faith and a humble desire
to be united with him, we will know the truth of God and his life
moving deeply in our hearts.

Let us be clear: This transformation by word and sacrament is
a work of God in us. It is impossible for us to achieve by ourselves.
God, the Holy One, must transform us inwardly as we respond to
his initiative. He alone can make us holy through the power of the
Spirit in us. Only the Spirit can teach us the truth and convince us
of it in a way that actually changes the way we think (John
16:8,13).

Jesus wants to sanctify us in the truth so that we can participate
in God's work of bringing salvation to the whole world (John 17:18).
Our goal should be to become a truer representation of Christ to the
world. Let us ask the Lord to set us apart for his purposes. Let us commit ourselves to proclaiming his truth through our words and
through our daily lives.

"Father, I want to be part of the great work of bringing salvation
to the world. Sanctify me in your word of truth. I consecrate my life
to your Son, Jesus. Purify me so that the world will see his presence
in me—his love, peace, joy, and humility. Let Christ in me be the
true manifestation of a sanctified life."

John 17:20-26

20 "I do not pray for these only, but also for those who believe in me through their word, 21 that they may all be one; even as you, Father, are in me, and I in you, that they also may be in us, so that the world may believe that you have sent me. 22 The glory which you have given me I have given to them, that they may be one even as we are one, 23 I in them and you in me, that they may become perfectly one, so that the world may know that you have sent me and have loved them even as you have loved me. 24 Father, I desire that they also, whom you have given me, may be with me where I am, to behold my glory which you have given me in your love for me before the foundation of the world. 25 O righteous Father, the world has not known you, but I have known you; and these know that you have sent me. 26 I made known to them your name, and I will make it known, that the love with which you have loved me may be in them, and I in them."

On the eve of his death, Jesus prayed for all who would believe in him through the apostles' message (John 17:20). He had us in mind, and of all the things he could have asked the Father to give us—steadfast faith, hope, love, power, courage—he prayed that we would have the same unity among ourselves that characterizes the life of the Trinity. Jesus' highest desire for us is that we would be one, as he and his Father are one (17:21).

When we live in the unity that Jesus intends for us, we know God's love, fellowship with him, and the power of his name. Jesus' purpose is broader than that, however. He calls us to communicate this unity to the world. He wants us to share with all men and women the good news that the intimate, loving relationship that he enjoys with the Father is possible for them, too. When we are united, the presence of Jesus—all the power of his name and the love of God—will be found in us.

This is the mission of the church, to share the gospel with all people. The Lord God, who is one, is himself the life that Jesus wants all men and women to have. As those called to bring that message to others, we must reflect the life and the unity that come from God alone.

Such unity, however, cannot be counterfeited by even our best efforts. The only way to achieve it is to look to Jesus' life and follow the way he established for us. The unity he had with the Father radiated throughout his life in his obedience to and reliance on God. To experience this kind of unity, we must open our hearts to Jesus and receive the blessings of unity, which is God's love for others manifested in lives transformed by the Spirit.

Let us examine our relationships and repent for the ways we allow, and even encourage, disunity in our families, communities, parishes, and places of work. Let us ask the Holy Spirit to show us where we are intolerant of others because of their race, religion, economic status, or even their appearance, dress or way of speaking. As we ask forgiveness, God himself will build up his church through our witness; his work will be furthered by our unity.

Glory on the Cross

JOHN
18:1–19:42

John 18:1-40

1   When Jesus had spoken these words, he went forth with his disciples across the Kidron valley, where there was a garden, which he and his disciples entered. 2 Now Judas, who betrayed him, also knew the place; for Jesus often met there with his disciples. 3 So Judas, procuring a band of soldiers and some officers from the chief priests and the Pharisees, went there with lanterns and torches and weapons. 4 Then Jesus, knowing all that was to befall him, came forward and said to them, "Whom do you seek?" 5 They answered him, "Jesus of Nazareth." Jesus said to them, "I am he." Judas, who betrayed him, was standing with them. 6 When he said to them, "I am he," they drew back and fell to the ground. 7 Again he asked them, "Whom do you seek?" And they said, "Jesus of Nazareth." 8 Jesus answered, "I told you that I am he; so, if you seek me, let these men go." 9 This was to fulfill the word which he had spoken, "Of those whom you gave me I lost not one." 10 Then Simon Peter, having a sword, drew it and struck the high priest's slave and cut off his right ear. The slave's name was Malchus. 11 Jesus said to Peter, "Put your sword into its sheath; shall I not drink the cup which the Father has given me?"

12   So the band of soldiers and their captain and the officers of the Jews seized Jesus and bound him. 13 First they led him to Annas; for he was the father-in-law of Caiaphas, who was high priest that year. 14 It was Caiaphas who had given counsel to the Jews that it was expedient that one man should die for the people.

15   Simon Peter followed Jesus, and so did another disciple. As this disciple was known to the high priest, he entered the court of the high priest along with Jesus, 16 while Peter stood outside at the door. So the other disciple, who was known to the high priest, went out and spoke to the maid who kept the door, and brought Peter in.

17 The maid who kept the door said to Peter, "Are not you also one

of this man's disciples?" He said, "I am not." [18] Now the servants and officers had made a charcoal fire, because it was cold, and they were standing and warming themselves; Peter also was with them, standing and warming himself.

[19] The high priest then questioned Jesus about his disciples and his teaching. [20] Jesus answered him, "I have spoken openly to the world; I have always taught in synagogues and in the temple, where all Jews come together; I have said nothing secretly. [21] Why do you ask me? Ask those who have heard me, what I said to them; they know what I said." [22] When he had said this, one of the officers standing by struck Jesus with his hand, saying, "Is that how you answer the high priest?" [23] Jesus answered him, "If I have spoken wrongly, bear witness to the wrong; but if I have spoken rightly, why do you strike me?" [24] Annas then sent him bound to Caiaphas the high priest.

[25] Now Simon Peter was standing and warming himself. They said to him, "Are not you also one of his disciples?" He denied it and said, "I am not." [26] One of the servants of the high priest, a kinsman of the man whose ear Peter had cut off, asked, "Did I not see you in the garden with him?" [27] Peter again denied it; and at once the cock crowed. [28] Then they led Jesus from the house of Caiaphas to the praetorium. It was early. They themselves did not enter the praetorium, so that they might not be defiled, but might eat the passover. [29] So Pilate went out to them and said, "What accusation do you bring against this man?" [30] They answered him, "If this man were not an evildoer, we would not have handed him over." [31] Pilate said to them, "Take him yourselves and judge him by your own law." The Jews said to him, "It is not lawful for us to put any man to death." [32] This was to fulfill the word which Jesus had spoken to show by what death he was to die.

[33] Pilate entered the praetorium again and called Jesus, and said to him, "Are you the King of the Jews?" [34] Jesus answered, "Do you say this of your own accord, or did others say it to you about me?"

³⁵ Pilate answered, "Am I a Jew? Your own nation and the chief priests have handed you over to me; what have you done?" ³⁶ Jesus answered, "My kingship is not of this world; if my kingship were of this world, my servants would fight, that I might not be handed over to the Jews; but my kingship is not from the world." ³⁷ Pilate said to him, "So you are a king?" Jesus answered, "You say that I am a king. For this I was born, and for this I have come into the world, to bear witness to the truth. Every one who is of the truth hears my voice." ³⁸ Pilate said to him, "What is truth?"

After he had said this, he went out to the Jews again, and told them, "I find no crime in him. ³⁹ But you have a custom that I should release one man for you at the Passover; will you have me release for you the King of the Jews?" ⁴⁰ They cried out again, "Not this man, but Barabbas!" Now Barabbas was a robber.

John 19:1-42

¹   Then Pilate took Jesus and scourged him. ² And the soldiers
plaited a crown of thorns, and put it on his head, and arrayed him in
a purple robe; ³ they came up to him, saying, "Hail, King of the
Jews!" and struck him with their hands. ⁴ Pilate went out again, and
said to them, "See, I am bringing him out to you, that you may know
that I find no crime in him." ⁵ So Jesus came out, wearing the crown
of thorns and the purple robe. Pilate said to them, "Behold the
man!" ⁶ When the chief priests and the officers saw him, they cried
out, "Crucify him, crucify him!" Pilate said to them, "Take him
yourselves and crucify him, for I find no crime in him." ⁷ The Jews
answered him, "We have a law, and by that law he ought to die,
because he has made himself the Son of God." ⁸ When Pilate heard
these words, he was the more afraid; ⁹ he entered the praetorium
again and said to Jesus, "Where are you from?" But Jesus gave no
answer. ¹⁰ Pilate therefore said to him, "You will not speak to me?
Do you not know that I have power to release you, and power to
crucify you?" ¹¹ Jesus answered him, "You would have no power over
me unless it had been given you from above; therefore he who
delivered me to you has the greater sin."
¹²   Upon this Pilate sought to release him, but the Jews cried out, "If
you release this man, you are not Caesar's friend; every one who
makes himself a king sets himself against Caesar." ¹³ When Pilate
heard these words, he brought Jesus out and sat down on the
judgment seat at a place called The Pavement, and in Hebrew,
Gabbatha. ¹⁴ Now it was the day of Preparation of the Passover; it
was about the sixth hour. He said to the Jews, "Behold your King!"
¹⁵ They cried out, "Away with him, away with him, crucify him!"
Pilate said to them, "Shall I crucify your King?" The chief priests
answered, "We have no king but Caesar." ¹⁶ Then he handed him
over to them to be crucified.

[17] So they took Jesus, and he went out, bearing his own cross, to the place called the place of a skull, which is called in Hebrew Golgotha. [18] There they crucified him, and with him two others, one on either side, and Jesus between them. [19] Pilate also wrote a title and put it on the cross; it read, "Jesus of Nazareth, the King of the Jews." [20] Many of the Jews read this title, for the place where Jesus was crucified was near the city; and it was written in Hebrew, in Latin, and in Greek. [21] The chief priests of the Jews then said to Pilate, "Do not write, 'The King of the Jews,' but, 'This man said, I am King of the Jews.'" [22] Pilate answered, "What I have written I have written."

[23] When the soldiers had crucified Jesus they took his garments and made four parts, one for each soldier; also his tunic. But the tunic was without seam, woven from top to bottom; [24] so they said to one another, "Let us not tear it, but cast lots for it to see whose it shall be." This was to fulfill the scripture, "They parted my garments among them, and for my clothing they cast lots."

[25] So the soldiers did this. But standing by the cross of Jesus were his mother, and his mother's sister, Mary the wife of Clopas, and Mary Magdalene. [26] When Jesus saw his mother, and the disciple whom he loved standing near, he said to his mother, "Woman, behold, your son!" [27] Then he said to the disciple, "Behold, your mother!" And from that hour the disciple took her to his own home.

[28] After this Jesus, knowing that all was now finished, said (to fulfill the scripture), "I thirst." [29] A bowl full of vinegar stood there; so they put a sponge full of the vinegar on hyssop and held it to his mouth. [30] When Jesus had received the vinegar, he said, "It is finished"; and he bowed his head and gave up his spirit.

[31] Since it was the day of Preparation, in order to prevent the bodies from remaining on the cross on the sabbath (for that sabbath was a high day), the Jews asked Pilate that their legs might be broken, and that they might be taken away. [32] So the soldiers came

and broke the legs of the first, and of the other who had been crucified with him; [33] but when they came to Jesus and saw that he was already dead, they did not break his legs. [34] But one of the soldiers pierced his side with a spear, and at once there came out blood and water. [35] He who saw it has borne witness—his testimony is true, and he knows that he tells the truth—that you also may believe. [36] For these things took place that the scripture might be fulfilled, "Not a bone of him shall be broken." [37] And again another scripture says, "They shall look on him whom they have pierced." [38] After this Joseph of Arimathea, who was a disciple of Jesus, but secretly, for fear of the Jews, asked Pilate that he might take away the body of Jesus, and Pilate gave him leave. So he came and took away his body. [39] Nicodemus also, who had at first come to him by night, came bringing a mixture of myrrh and aloes, about a hundred pounds' weight. [40] They took the body of Jesus, and bound it in linen cloths with the spices, as is the burial custom of the Jews. [41] Now in the place where he was crucified there was a garden, and in the garden a new tomb where no one had ever been laid. [42] So because of the Jewish day of Preparation, as the tomb was close at hand, they laid Jesus there.

The Hour Has Come

The Passion of Jesus in the Gospel of John

By Hallie Riedel

Jesus' hour finally had come. We now hear the teaching and witness the events that were the culmination of Jesus' purpose on earth. It was time for him to lay down his life, to endure the pain and humiliation of the cross. Yet, in a setting that one would expect to be filled with sadness and a sense of defeat, John depicts Jesus as marching triumphantly to his death, fully aware of the forces against him but equally aware of his purpose and in control of the events. As we watch the majestic Christ embrace his cross, we see the life that we can live as children of God—the life that he won for us as he poured out his blood.

Testifying to the Truth

From the very beginning of his passion, Jesus is portrayed by John as the One who takes the initiative. When Judas approaches with the soldiers and temple officers, Jesus confronts them and asks, "Whom do you seek?" (John 18:4). This is hardly the act of a man afraid for his life or one trying to evade his captors. Instead, John shows us Jesus taking advantage of the situation and revealing his true identity as the "I am"—a statement which literally floored his opponents (18:5). Again, when Peter tries to take matters into his own hands by striking the high priest's slave, Jesus rebukes him and reaffirms his determination to drink the cup the Father has given him (18:10-11).

Even during his interrogation by the high priest, when he has the opportunity to defend himself and explain his teachings to the religious authorities, Jesus chooses the road to the cross. Knowing that his interrogators are not open to the truth, he does not try to open a debate with them. Instead, he incites them further by reminding them of his followers and the way their lives had been changed by his teaching. His accusers are unable to accept the truth, however, and thus fall under the judgment of Jesus' own testimony.

All the while, as Jesus is bearing witness to the truth with stead-fast trust in God, his chief disciple, Peter, undergoes a similar test—and fails. While Peter doesn't vehemently reject Jesus, he does reveal an earthbound faith, a common theme in John's gospel. Fear for his life leads Peter to deny knowing Jesus, the one who at that very moment is giving an unswerving testimony that will lead to his death. Peter's emerging, though weak, faith is a clear sign that only the risen Lord—the one who speaks the truth from above—can bring us beyond our weaknesses and fears and enable us to give as pow-erful a testimony as Jesus gave.

Who Is on Trial?

By far the most complex scenes in John's passion account occur in the trial of Jesus before Pilate. John orchestrates these scenes to highlight Jesus' faithfulness to the truth and his ability to perceive the unfolding events from a heavenly perspective. Throughout the trial, John illuminates the contrast between the calm majesty of Jesus, the lack of resolve in Pilate, and the blind rage of the chief priests who stand accusing Jesus. John portrays the Roman procurator as con-stantly moving back and forth—"outside" the praetorium to speak with Jesus' enemies, and then "inside" to consult with Jesus.

The central scene "inside" the praetorium is the scourging of Christ. Here, all the earthly trappings of kingship are used in an attempt to mock Jesus, but in fact, are shown to be empty. In what is meant to be abject humiliation, Jesus' dignity and authority shine through, and Pilate becomes even more afraid. Even in this grueling test of faith, Jesus shows that his authority comes from above—something that only further infuriates his opponents and unnerves Pilate.

With each of Pilate's trips "outside" to speak with the Jews, with each hint that Pilate wants to release Jesus, the emotion and the hostility escalate. Finally, Pilate feels trapped into giving in to the demands of the Jews—the very thing that Jesus knew must happen for his Father's will to be accomplished.

The Irony of Death and Life

Irony pervades John's passion account, but nowhere is it more evident than during the trial. The refusal of Jesus' enemies to enter the praetorium for fear of defilement (John 18:28) shows itself to be absurd: They are at that moment handing him over to be put to death! With their demands that Jesus be crucified for making himself the Son of God (19:7), they not only unwittingly reveal Jesus' true identity, but show how hostile those unwilling to accept the truth can be. Finally, by proclaiming they "have no king but Caesar" (19:15), these religious leaders forfeit their identity as God's chosen people and align themselves instead with the oppressive Roman authorities.

Still, in the midst of this chaos, Jesus remains supremely aware of his mission and continues to move forward to his goal. He refers to himself as the one who reveals heavenly truth, and when Pilate shows that he cannot receive this truth, Jesus simply stops talking to him. Unlike the suffering servant whom the book of Isaiah portrays as keeping a humble silence, John paints Jesus' silence as a sign that Pilate has already passed judgment on himself. In the end, Pilate's deafness to the truth dictates the final result, and he hands Jesus over to be crucified.

Ironically, Pilate, the weak and fearful ruler, has "the last word" in the inscription he commands to be placed on the cross above Jesus. In a successful attempt to infuriate Jesus' accusers, he has the inscription read, "Jesus of Nazareth, King of the Jews" (John 19:19). However, while he does anger the Jews, he finally becomes the impartial judge he should have been at Jesus' trial. The verdict: Jesus is who he says he is, and his true identity is now on display for all passersby to witness. The irony is crowned in that, now crucified, Jesus fulfills his promise that by being "lifted up," he would draw all people to himself (12:31-32).

Behold, the Lamb of God!

John makes frequent use of Passover symbolism to portray Jesus as the true fulfillment of God's promises of deliverance—a deliverance that was foreshadowed when Moses led the Israelites out of Egypt and into the promised land. John sets the stage of the passion by placing events "before . . . the Passover, when Jesus knew that his hour had come" (John 13:1). He even specifies the timing of Jesus' trial so that Jesus is condemned at the very moment when the priests at the Temple were preparing the Passover lambs for sacrifice (19:14).

In response to Jesus' thirst on the cross, the Romans offer him a vinegar-soaked sponge attached to a stick made from a hyssop branch—the very kind of branch the Hebrews used to sprinkle the blood of the Passover lamb onto their door posts (John 19:28-29; Exodus 12:22). Finally, by telling us that the soldiers decided not to break Jesus' legs (John 19:36)—a customary practice in Roman crucifixion—John echoed Old Testament instructions that the Passover lamb be free from blemish and have no broken bones (Exodus 12:5,46). Jesus, heralded by John the Baptist as the "Lamb of God who takes away the sins of the world" (John 1:29), now reveals how sin will be lifted: by his death for our sake.

Completing a Mission of Love

Throughout the crucifixion scene, the words of Jesus from the cross reinforce his unwavering commitment to his mission and the intensity of his love for his people. What comfort in times of suffering to recall how faithful Jesus was to us, even in the midst of his terrible torments! The first poignant scene—between Jesus, his mother, and the beloved disciple—reminds us that essential to Jesus' mission was the establishment of the church. Mary, who stands for all faithful Jews longing for salvation, is entrusted to the beloved disciple, who symbolizes the community of believers. Thus, from the longing heart of the chosen people of God, the church is born and will thrive.

Having seen to the protection of his people in the church, Jesus acknowledges that "all was now finished" (John 19:28). Consequently, he cries out in thirst, wanting to drink to the end the "cup which the Father has given" (18:11). Even here, at the moment of death, Jesus makes a final act of commitment to the Father, athirst with love for us! Once he drinks the vinegar offered to him, Jesus declares, "It is finished" (19:30), and gives up his spirit. These final words echo statements Jesus made throughout his ministry that he had come to "complete" the works entrusted to him by the Father (4:34; 5:36; 17:4). The sacrifice is made. Sin is destroyed. The devil is defeated. God and man are united once more. John considers it only appropriate that Jesus end his life with a cry of triumph: "It is finished!"

The Fruit of the Cross

Only John's account of the passion describes any shedding of blood. To confirm Jesus' death, the soldiers pierce his side with a sword, which causes a flow of blood and water (John 19:34). This outpouring makes the effect of Jesus' death immediately visible: Through his saving death, Jesus has poured out new life upon the church. Now, anyone who looks on Jesus—"whom they have pierced" by their sins—can receive an overflowing measure of God's compassion and mercy (Zechariah 12:10).

The effects of the life that Jesus poured out from the cross also take flesh in the actions of Joseph of Arimathea and Nicodemus, both of whom had previously been less than shining examples of discipleship. Joseph was a "secret" disciple for fear of the Jews; and Nicodemus came to Jesus, but only in the cover of night (John 19:38–39). Now, however, the power of Jesus' death draws them both out into the open. Joseph takes the public step of asking Pilate permission to bury Jesus' body, and Nicodemus provides him with an extraordinary amount of spices, more suited to the burial of a king. As these two men make public their emerging faith in Jesus, they demonstrate the power of the fulfillment of God's promises in Christ.

John leaves out no opportunity to speak of the triumph of the cross. Even Jesus' burial in a borrowed grave foreshadows the coming resurrection: No permanent resting place for the victorious Son of God! In almost every line of his passion account, John is telling us that we can know the same closeness to the Father that Jesus knew. We can keep our eyes fixed on our heavenly goal. We can be cleansed daily from sin and delivered from bondage by the blood shed by Jesus, our Passover lamb. We can experience the life that Jesus poured out invigorating us and inspiring us to bear witness to Christ. In all things, his victory can be ours!

The Risen Christ

JOHN
20:1–21:25

John 20:1-10

¹ Now on the first day of the week Mary Magdalene came to the tomb early, while it was still dark, and saw that the stone had been taken away from the tomb. ² So she ran, and went to Simon Peter and the other disciple, the one whom Jesus loved, and said to them, "They have taken the Lord out of the tomb, and we do not know where they have laid him." ³ Peter then came out with the other disciple, and they went toward the tomb. ⁴ They both ran, but the other disciple outran Peter and reached the tomb first; ⁵ and stooping to look in, he saw the linen cloths lying there, but he did not go in. ⁶ Then Simon Peter came, following him, and went into the tomb; he saw the linen cloths lying, ⁷ and the napkin, which had been on his head, not lying with the linen cloths but rolled up in a place by itself. ⁸ Then the other disciple, who reached the tomb first, also went in, and he saw and believed; ⁹ for as yet they did not know the scripture, that he must rise from the dead. ¹⁰ Then the disciples went back to their homes.

From a sermon by St. Maximus, a fifth-century preacher and scholar who became bishop of Turin:

Christ is risen! He has burst open the gates of hell and let the dead go free; he has renewed the earth through the members of his Church now born again in baptism, and has made it blossom afresh with men brought back to life. His Holy Spirit has unlocked the doors of heaven, which stand wide open to receive those who rise up from the earth. Because of Christ's resurrection the thief ascends to paradise, the bodies of the blessed enter the holy city, and the dead are restored to the company of the living. There is an upward movement in the whole of creation, each element raising itself to something higher. We see hell restoring its victims to the upper regions, earth sending its buried dead to heaven, and heaven presenting the new arrivals to the Lord. In one and the same movement, our Savior's passion raises men from the depths, lifts them up from the earth, and sets them in the heights.

Christ is risen. His rising brings life to the dead, forgiveness to sinners, and glory to the saints. And so David the prophet summons all creation to join in celebrating the Easter festival: *Rejoice and be glad*, he cries, *on this day which the Lord has made*.

The light of Christ is an endless day that knows no night. Christ is this day, says the Apostle; such is the meaning of his words: *Night is almost over; day is at hand*. He tells us that night is almost over, not that it is about to fall. By this we are meant to understand that the coming of Christ's light puts Satan's darkness to flight, leaving no place for any shadow of sin. His everlasting radiance dispels the dark clouds of the past and checks the hidden growth of vice. The Son is that day to whom the day, which is the Father, communicates the mystery of his divinity. He is the day who says through the mouth of Solomon: *I have caused an unfailing light to rise in heaven*. And as in heaven no night can follow day, so no sin can overshadow the justice of Christ. The celestial day is perpetually bright and shining with brilliant light; clouds can never darken its skies. In the same way, the light of Christ is eternally glowing with luminous radiance and can never be extinguished by the darkness of sin. This is why John the evangelist says: *The light shines in the darkness, and the darkness has never been able to overpower it*.

And so, my brothers, each of us ought surely to rejoice on this holy day. Let no one, conscious of his sinfulness, withdraw from our common celebration, nor let anyone be kept away from our public prayer by the burden of his guilt. Sinner he may indeed be, but he must not despair of pardon on this day which is so highly privileged; for if a thief could receive the grace of paradise, how could a Christian be refused forgiveness?

John 20:11-18

11 But Mary stood weeping outside the tomb, and as she wept she stooped to look into the tomb; 12 and she saw two angels in white, sitting where the body of Jesus had lain, one at the head and one at the feet. 13 They said to her, "Woman, why are you weeping?" She said to them, "Because they have taken away my Lord, and I do not know where they have laid him." 14 Saying this, she turned round and saw Jesus standing, but she did not know that it was Jesus. 15 Jesus said to her, "Woman, why are you weeping? Whom do you seek?" Supposing him to be the gardener, she said to him, "Sir, if you have carried him away, tell me where you have laid him, and I will take him away." 16 Jesus said to her, "Mary." She turned and said to him in Hebrew, "Rab-boni!" (which means Teacher). 17 Jesus said to her, "Do not hold me, for I have not yet ascended to the Father; but go to my brethren and say to them, I am ascending to my Father and your Father, to my God and your God." 18 Mary Magdalene went and said to the disciples, "I have seen the Lord"; and she told them that he had said these things to her.

In confusion and grief, Mary Magdalene stood weeping outside Jesus' tomb. This Rabbi who had loved her as no one else had loved her was gone. Not only was he dead, his body was missing— apparently stolen away. Jesus had so touched her heart when he was alive that she wanted to honor him in his death by giving him a proper burial, and now even that was taken away from her. Would there be no end to this tragic series of events?

But Mary's sadness was to be short-lived. First there were angels; then a mysterious gardener; then, finally, the one thing she had so longed for and thought she would never hear again: his voice speaking her name (John 20:16). In an instant, everything changed. Jesus was alive! He was going not only to his Father, but to her Father. He had fulfilled his promise: God's love was poured out. Everyone could know God as a loving, merciful Father. Mary received all this as she heard Jesus speak her name and reveal himself to her.

This encounter was deeply personal. By speaking her name, Jesus touched her at the center of her heart, the place where all her fears lurked, the place where the struggle between the darkness of sin and the light of God's love was the fiercest. There, in the depth of her heart, Mary received the love of God, and her sadness was turned into a joy that moved her to tell the other disciples: "I have seen the Lord" (John 20:18). Only after Jesus spoke her name was she able to truly "see" him.

Mary's encounter with the risen Lord shows us what can happen in our own prayer as we quiet our hearts and listen for his voice. Every day, Jesus asks us to let him enter even the fears and darkness in our hearts—those places that we hide from the rest of the world—and heal them with his love. As he speaks our name, we too can say with Mary, "I have seen the Lord."

"Lord Jesus, I believe that you want to make yourself known to me just as intimately as you revealed yourself to Mary. By your Spirit, help me to listen so that when you speak my name I will be able to receive your love and proclaim your resurrection."

John 20:19-23

¹⁹ On the evening of that day, the first day of the week, the doors being shut where the disciples were, for fear of the Jews, Jesus came and stood among them and said to them, "Peace be with you." ²⁰ When he had said this, he showed them his hands and his side. Then the disciples were glad when they saw the Lord. ²¹ Jesus said to them again, "Peace be with you. As the Father has sent me, even so I send you." ²² And when he had said this, he breathed on them, and said to them, "Receive the Holy Spirit. ²³ If you forgive the sins of any, they are forgiven; if you retain the sins of any, they are retained."

Receive the Holy Spirit. (John 20:22)

Blessed Holy Spirit, you are God's presence within us, the faithful witness to God's mighty works and the enduring promise of things yet to come. Come, Breath of God, and dwell in us. By his death and resurrection, Jesus planted the seeds of eternal life. Now, through your presence, we know the first fruits of the harvest to come. In your love, strengthen us and prepare us for the coming wedding feast of Christ and his church.

Through you, O Spirit, God's word takes up residence in our hearts. You come to teach us God's laws and to transform us day by day. Through you, we who once were condemned to death for our trespasses are redeemed and forgiven. We who were burdened by sin can now walk in freedom. We who deserved no mercy can now extend mercy freely to others. Come, Comforter, and sustain us and encourage us in our daily walk. Help us understand the signs of the times. Be our teacher. Write the word of God on our hearts.

Come, faithful Counselor, and lead all nations to God. Fill the house of God with believers from every nation, race, and tongue. Make us into one body, united in our worship of the Lord. Prepare us, the bride, to take our place beside Jesus, our bridegroom. Overcome our natural differences as you did with the disciples and all those to whom they preached the gospel. Let everyone hear the good news in his or her native tongue and receive new life through you. Break down barriers that keep us apart. Give us compassion.

O great Advocate, teach us to pray in every circumstance and for every need. Move us to intercede for one another—even for our enemies. Form the prayers within us and give us the words to say. Give us the courage to speak the gospel in all situations and to all nations. Enable us to testify to the truth of Christ in our thoughts, words, and actions. Make us instruments of your grace, vessels of clay filled with your living water.

Come, Holy Spirit, reign within our hearts! Purify us and refine us! Empower us and use us! Live within us as you prepare us for our Heavenly Groom.

John 20:24-31

24 Now Thomas, one of the twelve, called the Twin, was not with them when Jesus came. 25 So the other disciples told him, "We have seen the Lord." But he said to them, "Unless I see in his hands the print of the nails, and place my finger in the mark of the nails, and place my hand in his side, I will not believe."
26 Eight days later, his disciples were again in the house, and Thomas was with them. The doors were shut, but Jesus came and stood among them, and said, "Peace be with you." 27 Then he said

to Thomas, "Put your finger here, and see my hands; and put out your hand, and place it in my side; do not be faithless, but believing." [28] Thomas answered him, "My Lord and my God!" [29] Jesus said to him, "Have you believed because you have seen me? Blessed are those who have not seen and yet believe." [30] Now Jesus did many other signs in the presence of the disciples, which are not written in this book; [31] but these are written that you may believe that Jesus is the Christ, the Son of God, and that believing you may have life in his name.

My Lord and my God! (John 20:28)

Filled with awe, Thomas uttered these words when he saw the risen Lord. Now he too could join his voice in the apostolic proclamation, "We have seen the Lord" (John 20:18,25). Thomas came to the same faith that transformed Mary Magdalene, Peter, John, and the others, and so was moved to make such a bold statement of faith and commitment to Jesus.

Thomas is a very important figure for us as we seek to deepen our faith. He stands as a hinge between the first Christians, who physically saw Jesus, and all the generations to come whose faith would rely on the apostles' witness and on their own vision of Christ with the "eyes of faith." Because Thomas first heard about the resurrection through his fellow apostles, and yet also had his own personal encounter with Christ, we can take his experience as a model for ourselves.

How can we deepen our faith? Like Thomas, we have the witness of the believing community, a two-thousand-year-old testimony of the people of God who continue to proclaim, "We have seen the Lord." This is no small matter, for while the gospel has penetrated every culture and age since the day of Pentecost, it retains its essential unity. The truth has not changed, and the promise of a personal encounter with Jesus remains as real as it did on the first Easter Sunday.

At the same time, like Thomas, we too are invited to experience something more than an agreement with the apostles' testimony: We can all experience the inner testimony of the Holy Spirit. This Spirit, whose role is to guide us into "all the truth" (John 16:13), was poured out so that we could know and experience the love of Christ in our hearts and freely embrace the salvation he offers.

The first community of believers lived a common life in which they knew the presence of their Savior and were drawn ever closer together in love and service. In their worship at the Eucharist, their attention to the apostles' teaching, their communal prayer, and their fellowship with one another, their faith deepened and the witness of their transformed lives touched others. In our prayer today, as we reflect on all that is available to us through the resurrection of Jesus and the power of the Spirit to reveal him to our hearts, let us sing with the psalmist: "Give thanks to the LORD, for he is good; his steadfast love endures for ever!" (Psalm 118:1).

John 21:1-14

[1] After this Jesus revealed himself again to the disciples by the Sea of Tiberi-as; and he revealed himself in this way. [2] Simon Peter, Thomas called the Twin, Nathan-ael of Cana in Galilee, the sons of Zebedee, and two others of his disciples were together. [3] Simon Peter said to them, "I am going fishing." They said to him, "We will go with you." They went out and got into the boat; but that night they caught nothing.

[4] Just as day was breaking, Jesus stood on the beach; yet the disciples did not know that it was Jesus. [5] Jesus said to them, "Children, have you any fish?" They answered him, "No." [6] He said to them, "Cast the net on the right side of the boat, and you will find some." So they cast it, and now they were not able to haul it in, for the quantity of fish. [7] That disciple whom Jesus loved said to Peter, "It is the Lord!" When Simon Peter heard that it was the Lord, he put on his clothes, for he was stripped for work, and sprang into the sea. [8] But the other disciples came in the boat, dragging the net full of fish, for they were not far from the land, but about a hundred yards off.

[9] When they got out on land, they saw a charcoal fire there, with fish lying on it, and bread. [10] Jesus said to them, "Bring some of the fish that you have just caught." [11] So Simon Peter went aboard and hauled the net ashore, full of large fish, a hundred and fifty-three of them; and although there were so many, the net was not torn. [12] Jesus said to them, "Come and have breakfast." Now none of the disciples dared ask him, "Who are you?" They knew it was the Lord. [13] Jesus came and took the bread and gave it to them, and so with the fish. [14] This was now the third time that Jesus was revealed to the disciples after he was raised from the dead.

The story of the miraculous catch of fish can teach us a good deal about fishing for people. The story that John recounts is similar to the great catch in Luke 5:1-11, yet it includes three specific emphases that only John gives us. He shows us that Jesus' call is universal; that he calls us to live in unity; and that we who have been called must share that call with others.

Some people are curious about why John specified the number of fish in the catch. Why 153? Many symbolic interpretations have been put forward, all pointing to the variety, size, and comprehensive nature of Jesus' call. St. Jerome said that since the zoology of his day specified 153 different kinds of fish, this number would symbolize a gathering in of people of all nations.

A more significant emphasis is placed on the fact that the disciples' nets didn't break, despite the size of the catch. By including this detail, John was illustrating the fact that despite the diversity and the number of followers, the Christian community need not be torn by divisions. This is a significant promise to hold on to, especially in the face of the church's turbulent history.

This miraculous story also has something to say about the commission of Jesus' followers to preach the gospel. Peter and the other disciples must have been flabbergasted by Jesus' charge to build the church. We can imagine them going out to fish in their restlessness—falling back on something they knew well how to do. But consider what the historical and spiritual implications would have been had they spent the rest of their lives trying to catch perch instead of people.

Something about this appearance of Jesus, however, launched them on their apostolic mission. Over the next thirty years (as described in the Acts of the Apostles), we never again hear of the apostles going out to fish. They were too busy bringing the gospel to the world. This is an important message for us as we come to faith in Christ. The life of Jesus in us does not remain just a personal and interior thing; it wells up within us and must be expressed to others.

"Jesus, continue to bring all people into the kingdom, that your will would be done on earth as it is in heaven. Strengthen your church today and help believers to love each other and live together in harmony. Lord, help us to be missionaries in whatever situations we find ourselves."

John 21:15-19

15 When they had finished breakfast, Jesus said to Simon Peter, "Simon, son of John, do you love me more than these?" He said to him, "Yes, Lord; you know that I love you." He said to him, "Feed my lambs." 16 A second time he said to him, "Simon, son of John, do you love me?" He said to him, "Yes, Lord; you know that I love you." He said to him, "Tend my sheep." 17 He said to him the third time, "Simon, son of John, do you love me?" Peter was grieved because he said to him the third time, "Do you love me?" And he said to him, "Lord, you know everything; you know that I love you." Jesus said to him, "Feed my sheep. 18 Truly, truly, I say to you, when you were young, you girded yourself and walked where you would; but when you are old, you will stretch out your hands, and another will gird you and carry you where you do not wish to go." 19 (This he said to show by what death he was to glorify God.) And after this he said to him, "Follow me."

Feed my sheep. (John 21:17)

Once again Peter stood warming himself by a charcoal fire. The last time we saw him in this position, he three times denied knowing Jesus (John 21:9; 18:18). In this scene, Jesus confronted him three times: "Do you love me?" (21:15,16,17). Still remembering the pain of his earlier denial (21:17), Peter answered "yes" each time. But Jesus did more than just reinstate this humbled apostle; he charged him to "Feed my sheep." What did Jesus see in Peter that he entrusted the future life and ministry of his church to him?

It was not Peter's wisdom that enabled him to care for Christ's followers as Jesus himself might. The issue was not pastoral gifts (though these gifts can be important) or Peter's leadership qualities that prompted Jesus to say, "Feed my sheep." No, the single quality that enabled Peter to care for Christ's followers was his love for Jesus: "Lord, you know that I love you" (John 21:16). Based on this foundation, how is someone who loves Jesus to respond to the Lord's charge to "Feed my sheep"? Andrew Murray, a pastor and prolific writer in South Africa during the nineteenth century, pondered the meaning of these three words: "Feed my sheep." Below is a summary of his insights:

To feed is to give to others what will help them grow. Every Christian must consider how to help others to grow: How can we explain Jesus' words so they might understand? How can we nurture a desire in them to turn to God?

The word *my* means that these sheep belong to Jesus. The work we do in caring for the Master's sheep involves hard work and initiative. But we must always remember that we nurture them for the Lord, not for the fulfillment of our own wishes or desires. They belong to him.

And what are sheep? Sheep depend upon their shepherds to create an environment that is safe, healthy, and good for their growth. A precious lot are weak and in constant need of care. In a similar way, all Christians are in one way or another sheep in need of care. We have a responsibility to care for them and feed them with the food Jesus gives.

"Lord Jesus, change my life and melt my heart with love for you. You have many sheep who need to be fed, and I want to take part in that work. May your love be the stimulus for what I do."

John 21:20-25

20 Peter turned and saw following them the disciple whom Jesus loved, who had lain close to his breast at the supper and had said, "Lord, who is it that is going to betray you?" 21 When Peter saw him, he said to Jesus, "Lord, what about this man?" 22 Jesus said to him, "If it is my will that he remain until I come, what is that to you? Follow me!" 23 The saying spread abroad among the brethren that this disciple was not to die; yet Jesus did not say to him that he was not to die, but, "If it is my will that he remain until I come, what is that to you?"

24 This is the disciple who is bearing witness to these things, and who has written these things; and we know that his testimony is true.

25 But there are also many other things which Jesus did; were every one of them to be written, I suppose that the world itself could not contain the books that would be written.

There are also many other things which Jesus did; were every one
of them to be written down, I suppose that the world itself could not
contain the books that would be written. (John 21:25)

How many books indeed! Jesus' actions—his miracles, healings, words, and deeds—are not limited to the few years during which he walked the earth. From the very beginning of
creation, the Son of God was at work—intervening in history and
preparing the world for his coming. Now, enthroned as Lord, his work
extends through the church as his people, filled with the Holy Spirit,
bring the light and life of the gospel to people everywhere.

We are all familiar with the biographies of the great saints of history: Francis of Assisi, Thérèse of Lisieux, Ignatius of Loyola, Edith
Stein, Vincent de Paul, and more. Yet how many "silent" saints have
there been—men and women whose stories have never been
recorded, yet whose lives are testimonies to the unending love and
grace of our Redeemer. Every citizen of the kingdom of heaven, both
past and present, is a book in himself or herself. In each one, God has
worked wonders. In ways great and small, Jesus never ceases his work,
so great is his love.

In the annals of history and in the homes of families throughout
the ages, God has always been at work. His desire is that everyone
come to know the life that is available through his Son, Christ Jesus.
When we sinned and turned away from God, he sent his Son, the
very one through whom and for whom we were made, to redeem us.
Offering himself on the cross to ransom us from darkness, Jesus performed his greatest work of all. Now, through faith and baptism into
his death and resurrection, all people can receive his life within them
and become yet another "book," another testimony to the love and
power of God.

Let us open our hearts to Jesus, the author of our lives and per-
fecter of our faith. Let us give him reign over our thoughts and actions

so that he can write yet another book of testimony within us. Let us proclaim the gospel to others, that the witness of our lives would be like an open book before them, inviting them to receive the same grace that we—and all the saints—have received.

Topical Index of John's Gospel

Events in the Life of Jesus:

Significant Characters in the Gospel:

Other Resources from The Word Among Us Press

Also from the Gospel Devotional Commentary Series:
Matthew: A Devotional Commentary
Mark: A Devotional Commentary
Luke: A Devotional Commentary
Leo Zanchettin, General Editor

Enjoy reading and praying through the gospels with commentaries that include each passage of scripture with a faith-filled meditation.

Books on the Saints:
A Great Cloud of Witnesses—The Stories of 16 Saints and Christian Heroes by Leo Zanchettin and Patricia Mitchell

I Have Called You by Name—The Stories of 16 Saints and Christian Heroes by Patricia Mitchell

Each book contains practical, down-to-earth biographies along with selections of the saints' own writings and time lines to provide historical context.

The Wisdom Series:
The writings from these spiritual masters become more accessible to the contemporary reader in The Word Among Us Wisdom series. These popular books include short biographies of the authors and selections from their writings grouped around themes such as prayer, forgiveness, and mercy.

Welcoming the New Millennium, Wisdom from Pope John Paul II

My Heart Speaks, Wisdom from Pope John XXIII

Live Jesus! Wisdom from Saints Francis de Sales and Jane de Chantal

A Radical Love, Wisdom from Dorothy Day

Love Songs, Wisdom from St. Bernard of Clairvaux

Walking with the Father, Wisdom from Brother Lawrence

Touching the Risen Christ, Wisdom from the Fathers

To order call 1-800-775-9673 or order online at www.wau.org